May 17,

98¢ Goodwell

ALL THE RAGE

CHARLES HALEY

with Joe Layden

ALL THE RAGE

The Life of an NFL Renegade

Andrews McMeel
Publishing

Kansas City

www.andrewsmcmeel.com

LIBRARY OF CONGRESS CATALOGING-IN-PUBLICATION DATA

Haley, Charles, 1964–
    All the rage : the life of an NFL renegade / Charles Haley with Joe Layden.
        p.   cm.
    ISBN 0-8362-3587-8 (hardcover)
    1. Haley, Charles, 1964– . 2. Football players—United States—Biogra-
phy. 3. Dallas Cowboys (Football team) I. Layden, Joseph,
1959– . II. Title.
GV939.H265A3   1997
796.332 ' 092—dc21
[B] ,   97-14994
                                                          CIP

Designed by Kathryn Parise
Composition by Hillside Studio, Inc.

This book is dedicated to
Princess, Charles Jr., and Brianna. I love you.
—C.H.

For my father,
who likes a good story almost as much
as he likes a good football game.
— J.L.

CONTENTS

CONTENTS

ACKNOWLEDGMENTS

I would not have been able to write this book about some very emotionally charged periods in my life without the love and support of my wife, Karen. A very special thank-you to Karen for believing in me.

To my parents, Mr. and Mrs. George Haley Sr., for your unconditional love, faith, and support. To my in-laws, Mr. and Mrs. Silas Smith Jr., for all your prayers.

My children, Princess, Charles Jr., and Brianna, too, helped me through the challenging times that are documented in this book. Thanks for all the hugs and kisses. To my godchildren, Gari and Donavan—reach for the stars! To my siblings, James, George Jr., Lawrence, and David, for always being there.

To my attorney and agent, Kurt Robinson, for your early encouragement and commitment to making it all happen. You have provided much guidance during my eleven years in the NFL. To Joe Layden, for your time and patience during the writing process. Thanks for making the sessions so comfortable. I am grateful for your insight in making my words come alive. To Frank Weimann of The Literary Group—I appreciate your belief in the project. To Jake Morrissey of Andrews McMeel, for the willingness and courage to publish this book.

To my accountant, Mike Steele, for keeping the numbers straight and taking care of business promptly. To my financial advisor, Bob Gist, for showing me the smart way to invest my money—diversification!

To the coaches at James Madison University. Especially Challace McMillin, Jimmy Prince, and Danny Wilmer, for strengthening me. I am grateful for your insight and frequent reminders of the task at hand.

To the great Bill Walsh for your unbelievable vision and dedication. Thanks for the early encouragement. To coaches Bill McPherson and Tommy Hart for making me a better player. Also, thanks to Dwaine Board and Michael Carter for showing me the ropes during my early years with the San Francisco 49ers.

To Jerry Jones and Stephen Jones for accepting me, letting me just do my job, and allowing me the opportunity to win three more Super Bowls. To coach Barry Switzer for showing me the importance of family. To Rich Dalrymple for helping me communicate better.

To teammates Ronnie Lott, Joe Montana, Eric Wright, Jerry Rice, Michael Carter, Gary Clark, Troy Aikman, Emmitt Smith, Deion "Prime Time" Sanders, Michael Irvin, Tony Tolbert, Leon Lett, and Godfrey Myles—you guys do it like nobody else. Thanks for being prepared and ready to play on Sundays. Thanks for all the memories.

To John Madden—you are the greatest!

To the people who watch and support the game of football—I love you all.

—Charles Haley
May 1997

CHAPTER 1

Are We Having Fun Yet?

On December 3, 1995, I played what I thought was my last professional football game. The nagging pain in my back had been growing more intense. Some days I could barely get out of bed in the morning. A combination of adrenaline, Vicodin, novocaine, and pride had carried me through twelve games. But now I was hitting the wall. Actually, the wall was hitting me.

We were playing the Washington Redskins at Texas Stadium. The third play of the game was a running play toward my side at defensive end. Their tackle and tight end came up to double-team me. I threw the tight end off, just like I had a hundred other times. But the tackle really got into me, straightened me up, pushed me off balance. Then I saw the ball carrier. Just a flash. He ran right up my chest, knocked me backward. That's when I felt it—like a white-hot razor slicing into my lower back.

I got up after the play, but I knew right away that some-thing was seriously wrong. I shuffled to the sideline and gulped a couple Vicodin, because I thought that would help. No chance. It didn't even put a dent in the pain. But you know what? I played the rest of the first half. I wasn't going to go out like that. I didn't want the last play of my career to be an injury. I thought if I just kept moving, kept playing, maybe I'd be OK. I was lying to myself, though. I had injured my back once before. I'd had surgery to remove a ruptured disk in 1994, so I knew what it was like. This was a similar feeling, only much worse.

By halftime I could barely walk. A couple guys had to lit-erally push me up the tunnel into the locker room, because I couldn't move my legs. I knew it was over then. I wouldn't be able to play in the second half. I probably wouldn't play the rest of the season. And then a thought entered my mind. A frightening thought:

I'll never play again.

I won't lie to you. It hit me hard. I sat in the middle of that locker room and thought about all I had been through. I thought about what it meant to be a professional football player, and what it meant to be a Dallas Cowboy. I thought about how much of my life had been devoted to the game. And I started to cry. I cried like a baby, because I thought my career was over. That might sound kind of strange, consider-ing that I had nearly retired a year earlier. But that was dif-ferent. Then I was thinking about leaving on my own terms. Now I was being forced out. Now I was a loser.

Halftime ended. The players went back out on the field. I

stayed behind. I sat in the locker room, all alone, listening to the roar of the crowd, listening to the game, feeling it, like thunder . . . crying my ass off.

If you had asked me before the 1995 season what type of year the Dallas Cowboys were going to have, I would have said, "Great!" I mean, we were loaded, man. When you have Troy Aikman at quarterback, Michael Irvin at wide receiver, and Emmitt Smith in the backfield, you have an offense that's just about unstoppable. And our defense was even better. We had the best defense I'd ever been on. We had so much talent that we should have been untouchable.

Most people would probably say that we did have a good season. After all, we won the Super Bowl. But I'm a competitor. With the talent that we had, we did not go out and perform up to our capabilities. We should have dominated people. We should have been attacking and going after folks. Instead we laid back and fell prey to a lot of teams. We lost four games that season. We shouldn't have lost any.

I'll tell you something else, and I believe this with all my heart: If we had played the San Francisco 49ers in the NFC Championship Game, they would have beaten us. If the Packers hadn't knocked them off, there would have been no Super Bowl XXX for the Cowboys, because the 49ers would have kicked our asses. When you play a team like the 49ers, you have to be able to adapt and change on the fly. Our defensive coaches couldn't do that. They couldn't function under that kind of pressure. Week after week I would sit through meetings, bitching and moaning, telling those motherfuckers that they needed to change stuff. And they'd say, "Well, gee, it's been working since we brought it in here. Why should we change now?" And I'd just look at them and think, *What the fuck do you think the rest of the coaches in this league are doing? You think they aren't doing their homework? You think they aren't trying to figure out how to beat you?*

When you lose a football game, there are only a few places you can lay blame. If there's a lack of effort or poor technique, it's the players' fault. But when you're talking about schemes . . . that's the coaches' responsibility. The coaches have to make sure that the players are in the right place and let them use their abilities. So, all season long, it was like, *We know what's coming at us, and the coaches know what's coming at us. But we can't stop it because we don't have people with vision.*

For me, the trouble began in training camp. We had a new defensive coordinator, Dave Campo, and there was a lack of communication between him and John Blake, our defensive line coach. I thought Campo was all right as a secondary coach (which is what he used to be), but there's a big difference between coaching the defensive backs and running the whole defense. To be honest, I really didn't think Campo knew what the hell he was doing. So we never hit it off. In fact, we still don't hit it off.

I had played really well in 1994, and my back felt strong going into camp. I was in the best shape I could possibly have been in. But I wanted to be careful. The whole game plan was supposed to be set. I had discussed it with the coaching staff, including Barry Switzer, the head coach. We all agreed that I wouldn't do much during camp, so that I would be healthy when the season began. But once we got into training camp, some of the assistant coaches started pushing me. I don't mean they were saying, "Charles, get your ass out there!" It doesn't work that way in the NFL. Instead, they play psychological games with you. They'd walk by and mumble a lot, maybe say, "Charles, feel like practicing today?" After a while it really got on my damn nerves. You see, I'm not afraid of hard work. I thought I was doing the right thing. I was trying to save myself for the season so that I could earn the money they were paying me—which, by the way, was quite a lot: $12 million over four years. Come September, I did not want to be standing on the sidelines.

Looking back, I realize now that I should have been stronger. I should have insisted on doing nothing but conditioning the first few weeks of training camp. Then I could have worked my way into pad drills. But no contact.

Instead, they broke me down. Eventually I just said, "Fine, I'll give them what they want. I'll practice. I'll play all the preseason games." And, of course, I got all banged up. We won a Super Bowl that year, but 1995–96 was one of the hardest, longest, and most difficult seasons of my career. There was never a moment when the injuries did not bother me. I was in excruciating pain from the opening kick of the first game. And it never got better.

The week before our season opener against the Giants I

agreed to go through "pain management." I had expected some sort of useless, bullshit therapy involving psychological gimmicks. Uh-uh. Instead I found myself on a table, half asleep, sedatives coursing through my veins. Dr. Robert Haynesworth, a physician at Baylor University Medical Center in Dallas, inserted a long needle in my back. I had a disk problem, and this was supposed to alleviate the pain. I don't even know what he was injecting (sometimes I think it's better not to ask), but it did give me relief for a little while. Unfortunately, I also had tendinitis in my right knee, and sometimes I had to take a needle for that, too—just to be able to play. The doctors would inject a cocktail of anti-inflammatory medication and painkillers. A lot of weeks I couldn't function without it.

On opening day, though, I was there. All shot up and ready to go. We beat the Giants, 35–0, on a Monday night in East Rutherford, New Jersey. Emmitt scored four touchdowns, and we held the Giants to just sixty-five yards on offense.

Our defense was capable of that sort of performance. And when Deion Sanders—the best cornerback in the league—arrived as a free agent a few days later, we became even stronger. Still, there were a lot of frustrating moments between that first Monday night game and the Super Bowl.

October 4, 1995

Another day in Dallas, another shitstorm. And, as usual, it swirled around me.

A few days earlier, in Washington, we had lost to the Redskins by a score of 27–23. We were five weeks into the new season, and we had lost just once. Not bad. Unless you're the Dallas Cowboys, of course. America's Team is not supposed to lose. Ever.

I had stayed behind after the game to visit friends and family in Virginia. I needed a break. My back—surgically repaired eighteen months earlier—was acting up again. I had a groin injury that made every step painful. And my knees ached. In general, I was a mess. I was thirty-one years old . . . going on fifty. But I kept telling myself I'd be OK. Just take a couple days off, pop a few more Vicodin, get a little treatment later in the week, and I'd be ready to play. That was the cycle for a lot of guys in the NFL, and I accepted it.

What I could not accept were the words I was now hearing; words that tore into my heart. On Monday afternoon, while I was recuperating in Virginia, Barry Switzer had ripped me a new asshole. Barry, you have to understand, is normally a pretty decent guy. If anything, he'd been too soft on players during his first year and a half in Dallas. Apparently, though, in the wake of our first loss of the season, he had decided to adopt a different approach.

Barry and the other coaches had reviewed the game film, the way they always do. They watched the Redskins kick our butts all over RFK Stadium, and they were appropriately offended. Somehow, though, they came to the conclusion that my performance at defensive end deserved special recognition. One of the defensive coaches went to Barry and said something like, *"Charles is doing his own thing again. And he's got other guys on the defense following him."* So Barry decided he had to run us through the mud. He met with the team. Then he met with the media. And, man, did he give those vultures something to chew on.

That's what I was hearing now, as I sat in the locker room on Wednesday morning. Some of the guys on the D-line were telling me the story. To be honest, I had trouble believing it. But they had saved the newspaper. So I started to read. I was stunned. There was Barry, trashing not only me, but also Tony Tolbert, our other defensive end, and Leon Lett, a defensive tackle. Two of my closest friends. I looked at the words—*"embarrassingly poor technique . . . disregarded their responsibilities . . . defensive lapses"*—and I felt the anger rising in my throat.

If you're going to dog me, goddammit, at least do me the courtesy of talking to me first! My back was killing me. I pulled my damn groin. But you know what? I played anyway! And now you're going to sit there and ridicule me? In the press? I'm not buying any of that.

I have never been afraid of confrontation, on or off the playing field. Football, to me, is about respect. You earn respect through your actions, through your accomplishments, through your talent. I have five Super Bowl rings—more than any other player in the history of the game. I've played in five Pro Bowls. I have sweated blood for every team I've represented, including the Dallas Cowboys. I believed then and I believe now that Barry handled that situation badly. He's the coach, of course, and he has the right to criticize his players. But he should have talked to me first—man to man. What he did was bullshit! He showed no respect for me whatsoever.

And that's precisely what I told him. Like I said, I don't mind confrontation. I don't mind getting in someone's face. Because that is my approach to life, I have a lot of enemies and only a few friends. But I have my pride. My dignity. You do what you have to do, right? And what I had to do that day, immediately, was speak with the coaching staff. I met with Barry. I met with John Blake. And I met with Dave Campo. I met with every damn one of them, and I told them, "This is not the way it's supposed to be!" You see, I'm not like them. I'm not going to just run to the media and let them read my comments in the newspapers. They'll hear it from me first.

Barry offered a public apology the next day. "I made a mistake," he said. "And I'm man enough to admit it. When we lose, we lose as a team. It's wrong for me to cite individual players."

I was glad to hear him say that, but I was still pissed off. In fact, I was seething. One thing I've learned about myself is that I have a lot of hate in my body, and sometimes it just builds up to where it has to be released. I've tried to use workouts and football and running as a release for my anger, but it doesn't always work. Part of it, I guess, comes from not being able to forgive people. I try to channel my anger and not speak out as much as I used to, not let people get to me. But every so often I just blow up. I don't know . . . I probably need to go through a stress management program or something.

———————

Our next opponents were the Green Bay Packers. I didn't practice much that week, in the days leading up to the game. The coaches kept telling me, "If you're hurt, don't play." Well, what the hell was that supposed to mean? *If* you're hurt. Man, they *knew* my back was killing me. But I was going to give it my best shot. I wanted to rest during the week and see how I felt on Sunday. But now it was like a mind game or something. They wanted me to prove that I was ready to play by practicing, which was ridiculous. I'd been in the league ten years. I knew my body. I knew what I had to do to get ready for a game. They made me so mad that I just said, "Fuck it! I won't play." In the end, though, I decided to dress. I figured, if somebody goes down, then I'll play.

Well, things did not go exactly as I had planned. We were in trouble right from the start. Our defense wasn't stopping anything. We couldn't get to Brett Favre, the Packers' quarterback. And if you can't stop Brett Favre, you can't stop the Packers. Pretty soon everybody started getting on my case. Troy Aikman was talking shit to me every time he came off the field. You hear about Troy being quiet and everything, but the truth is, he'll speak his mind. Troy's about winning. That's all there is to it. So he kept walking by, making faces, and saying, "I hope you're happy." I tried to ignore him. But then Darryl Johnston, our fullback, started in. And Michael Irvin . . . *The Playmaker!* All guys on offense, which figures. They'd walk by, talk more shit, really give it to me. And I was just standing there, eating sunflower seeds, trying to ignore it. Eventually I said, "OK, I'll play. Just leave me the fuck alone."

I entered the game early in the second quarter. I played the rest of the half, the whole third quarter, and a little bit of the fourth. Maybe forty plays total. We ended up winning the game, but I took little satisfaction in the victory. I was still mad. I was hurt—emotionally and physically. Much of my frustration was vented through the media. In retrospect, that was probably a mistake, although I said nothing I hadn't already said to the coaching staff. Still, when your words appear in print the next day, they do take on greater weight:

THEY'LL NEVER GET ME BACK IN THIS UNIFORM AGAIN!

I meant it at the time, man. I just felt like a knife had been stuck in my back, and I was not going to let them twist it. I was not going to stay there and let them keep stabbing me. So I made a decision. It wasn't just talk. I figured I was out of there when the season was over. I'd either retire or ask for a trade. Of course, the media got that all wrong. They made it sound like I was going to quit right on the spot. I would never do that. I had a contract. And I honor my contracts.

Fortunately, it never came to that. Barry and I were able to sit down the next day and talk. He apologized to me and I apologized to him. I just wanted him to know that there couldn't be a double standard. If they've got something they want to say about me, then bring me in and let's talk about it. Let's air it out. But I don't like getting off a plane and having people say, "Damn! What's up with you and your coach?" Especially when I don't know what the hell they're talking about.

Eventually I was able to put it behind me, because I didn't have any other choice. In the NFL, you do your job. Or you don't have a job. Fortunately, it's easy for me to get lost in my work because I like to do it. I don't really care whether the coaches *like* me or not. That's irrelevant. The bottom line is, I can play football; I know how to win. There's one man who makes the final decision on the Dallas Cowboys, and that's the owner, Jerry Jones. If he doesn't want me on the team anymore, then I'll be gone. But until that happens, I'll keep doing my job.

I hold Dave Campo responsible for most of the problems we had in '95. Maybe I'm being too harsh, but that's the way I feel. When I think of the defensive coaches I've really admired and respected—guys like Dave Wannstedt and Butch Davis—Campo just doesn't measure up. Those guys weren't afraid. They had *balls*. That's why I loved playing for them. If we were winning by 20, we were still coming at you. If we were losing by 20, we were still coming at you. With those guys, if we went down, we went down shooting every bullet.

But it wasn't like that anymore. The San Francisco game was probably the best example—and one of the low points of the year. It was the tenth week of the season, and a lot of people were calling it a preview of the NFC title game. But it turned out to be a complete mismatch. We were down 31–7 at halftime. I mean, we were getting the living shit kicked out of us. And when we went into the locker room, the first words out of Campo's mouth were: "You guys are not giving enough effort." I couldn't believe it. I was looking at this guy, and I was thinking, *Not enough effort? This team is driving all over us. We're dying out there, man, and that's the best you can say? Not enough effort? For Christ's sake, their scheme is beating us!* I kept waiting for him to walk over to the chalkboard and draw up another defense. I kept waiting for him to do . . . something. But no. He just kept talking.

Not enough effort.

So we went back out in the second half and did the same thing. And they continued to hammer us. We never did get back in that game. The 49ers humiliated us, 38–20. It was only our second loss of the year. But it felt, to me, like the season was slipping away.

Charles in Charge, Part I
NAKED LUNCH

There are things I do for no particular reason; things I'm going to do whether people like it or not; things I can't necessarily explain. Mannerisms, I guess you'd call them. Like talking trash. Before practice, during practice, after practice—I'm a motormouth. And I have my own internal clock, which always seems to be a few minutes slow. I'm late for meetings. I'm late getting out on the field. That doesn't mean I don't want to work. It just means that I like messing with the people in authority. I'm always on the borderline with the assistant coaches. I drive those motherfuckers crazy. If they didn't get all worked up about it, I probably wouldn't even bother. But seeing them fume is half the fun.

Sometimes, just to see how people will react, I'll go to a defensive line meeting wearing nothing but a towel wrapped around my head. No shorts, no shirt, no shoes. It's the jokester in me. He's been a part of my life since I was a little boy, and sometimes he just has to come out and say hello. I can't stop him.

It's not about being irresponsible. And it doesn't

14

mean I don't take the game seriously; I do. In fact, I don't know many players who work harder to stay in shape than I do; who want to win more than I do. Maybe that's the point. To me, it's a form of competition, a way to challenge the people in charge. When an assistant coach does something you don't like, you have to deal with it. And there are several options. You can blow up and yell and scream, which I've done, but that rarely accomplishes anything. Or you can try to drive the son of a bitch crazy. As I've gotten older, I've come to appreciate the latter approach. If a coach is acting like an asshole—or even if he simply doesn't know what the hell he's doing—I'll do things to piss him off, to confuse him. I'll play games with him, see what I can and can't get away with. See, it's always been that way with me, in football and in life: If I step out of bounds, somebody better kick my foot back in or there's going to be a new boundary. A lot of coaches don't understand me, because I do a lot of crazy stuff. But it's just the way I am.

I like to play pranks on people. Silly, juvenile pranks. Once in a while on film day, for example, I might go in and dismantle the video equipment. Then the assistant coaches come in and get all pissed off. By the time they get all the cables connected properly, we don't have any time left.

To be honest, though, I liked it better when we had the old film projectors, the ones that made a lot of noise. The lights would go down and you'd hear that . . . *click!* . . . and then the projector would start whirring. After a while you couldn't even hear the coaches talking. All you'd hear is the projector: *Hmm-mmmmm.* Like a fan on a summer night, man. I don't care who you are—twenty minutes of that and you're out cold. Most of the time the coaches would be on the lookout for players who fell asleep, and they'd come down hard on you. With me, though, it was like, *Let him sleep. At least he won't be raising hell.*

CHAPTER 2

Mom Kicks a Little Ass

Gladys, Virginia, is a small town—so small they have to pump in sunlight, as we say in the South. When I was growing up, there wasn't a whole lot to do, except work and go to school and play sports. TV wasn't a factor in our lives, the way it is in kids' lives today; for a long time, we couldn't even afford a television set.

The sad thing was, my parents worked their asses off. They just never had much to show for it. My father, George Haley, was a machine operator for a fiberglass company; he cut pulp wood on the side. Mom—Virginia Haley—worked for the Lane Company, a furniture manufacturer. She was a sprayer. It was tough, assembly-line work. She'd stand there all day, watching pieces of furniture rolling by, spraying them with paint or varnish or whatever. Mom was meticulous. Still is.

She was the disciplinarian of the family. She laid down the rules and made sure they were enforced. Mom believed in spanking. She used switches, and man did they hurt. If you got out of line, she'd just say, "You do what I'm telling you to do —or else we're going outside!" And that was the end of it. Unless you were stupid enough to challenge her.

My mother was not a little woman. She was about five-ten, 180 pounds, and she never took crap from anyone—not from me, not from my brothers, not from my dad. No one. To this day, if we have a family argument of some kind, and one of us gets in her face, she won't back down. My father was a big guy, scary, about six-two, 250 pounds. But you know what? I think he spanked me maybe once or twice my whole life. Mom took care of that.

And you know what else?

I love her to death.

Mom never let us out at night. During the day, though, it was a different story. She didn't want us hanging around the house. She believed strongly that boys should be outside, running around, playing sports. Tiring themselves out. That was fine by me, since I loved sports, especially football. Even though we lived in the country, finding enough kids to play was never a problem, since we were practically a team by ourselves: the five Haley boys. James was the firstborn. Then came George Jr. and Lawrence. I was number four, born on January 6, 1964. My little brother David came along one year later.

We were big kids, country kids, and we liked to play pickup football against different neighborhoods. What we'd do is hustle them, let them run for three quarters, maybe score a couple touchdowns. Then we'd just break them up. This was tackle football, no pads. None of that candy-ass, two-hand touch shit for us. We played the real deal in dirt fields, vacant lots, parking lots . . . wherever we could find an empty space. You had to know how to land, because there were rocks and broken glass everywhere. Kids would come into our neighborhood and we'd set them up: One of us would take the head, the other would take the feet. We used to get a lot of people that way. I know that sounds cruel, but that's the way we played. We were blood in those games—me and my brothers and all our kinfolk against anyone who dared to challenge us. Other teams would walk into our neighborhood expecting just another football game, and we'd send them home in an ambulance.

We were proud of it, too. It was us against the world. There's nothing like playing football with family. It makes it special.

Of course, playing *against* family is a different story. The only time I ever got hurt in a sandlot game was when I was in elementary school. We were right outside the school, during recess, and the game was supposed to end when the school bell rang. Just as the bell sounded, Lawrence tripped me—deliberately, I might add—and I fell into a ditch and broke my shoulder. I was eleven years old, maybe twelve, and it was the most painful thing I had ever experienced. It was my first injury, and it made me realize just how brutal a sport football can be. Looking back, I guess it was like an indoctrination—

preparation for all of the violence and suffering I would encounter down the road.

The truth is, though, I got off on it: I was proud of that first injury; it was my personal medal of honor. Of course, the thing I liked best about football was *hitting*—not getting hit. I was an aggressive kid, an energetic kid, and football seemed to be a respectable outlet for all that energy. I played basketball while I was growing up, too. But football was my love. The tough kids in town played football; the weak kids played basketball. I wanted to be a tough kid. Like I said, though, Gladys is not exactly a thriving metropolis, so a lot of kids played both sports. It wasn't like today, where kids specialize in a sport and attend camps to improve their skills, and study tapes of their favorite players, all in the hope of getting a college scholarship or playing pro ball. I never thought of any of that when I was a kid. I didn't follow sports at all; I just played sports.

Religion was an important part of my childhood, too. We practically lived in the church when I was growing up. For me, everything started with church, with God. I didn't want to be a big-time professional ballplayer when I was a little boy; I wanted to be a preacher. I used to watch those Southern Baptist preachers come strolling into a church, man, and they'd look so sharp, so confident. They'd get the congregation going, take charge, lift everyone's spirits, just by talking. They had such power, such conviction. I really admired that. Maybe that's why I like to talk so much today. Maybe that's why my mouth gets me in trouble sometimes.

Anyway, I never had football posters or trading cards or any of that crap. I had my mom. She kept me straight. In fact, if she hadn't played such a strong role in my life, I wouldn't be here today. I'd be in jail . . . or dead. I'm sure of that. Mom straightened all of us out when we got in trouble. The thing was, in public, she'd always back me up, fight for me, whether I was right or wrong. She just felt that was the right thing to do, and she loved me. But then we'd get home and she'd tear my butt up.

It was my mother who made me realize my potential as a football player. Honest to God. See, when I was a freshman at William Campbell High School, and I was on the junior varsity team, I wasn't playing very much. I was the class clown then—always going for laughs, fooling around, playing practical jokes and stuff. Unlike today, though, I didn't work very hard and I didn't take the game seriously. I didn't deserve to play. I'll tell you something else, something that was hard for me to admit at the time: I was scared. When I was little, playing sandlot games with my brothers and cousins, we always knew we were going to win; all we had to do was name the score. This was different. At this level I didn't know what to expect. Suddenly I was getting hit a lot—by kids who were bigger and stronger than me. If I didn't play, I didn't have to worry about getting hit. So I stopped caring.

Mom didn't understand any of this, primarily because I never told her. She just thought her son was getting screwed by the coach. So, one day, just before halftime, she came marching down out of the bleachers and confronted the JV coach. At first I didn't even notice her there. We were all start-ing to head for the end zone for the halftime talk, so I was walking in the other direction. But then I heard this commo-tion, and I looked back. And there was Mom, getting in the coach's face, screaming, chewing him out. I was stunned, but I was also curious, so I moved closer. Eventually, I could hear my mother's voice.

"Why ain't my son in the game? I came all the way out here to see my sons play and I want to see them play—all of them!"

My brother, Lawrence, who had no sympathy for me, rushed right to the coach's defense.

"He's not playing, Mom, because all he does is fool around."

The coach started trying to explain, but my mother wouldn't let him get in a word. She wouldn't hear none of it. She just kept on yelling and waving her arms. Finally she said, "Tell me what Charles has to do, and he'll do it. I promise." Then they talked a little more and my mom walked away.

I didn't know what to expect when I got home. I didn't know if she'd be happy, mad, or what. I just know that I was really embarrassed that I had put her in that situation. The truth is, I *belonged* on the bench—the coach was right. But she stood up for me anyway. It was the most amazing thing. I didn't even know she cared that much. She had other kids who were all doing great things. I was the fuck-up, and yet she still supported me. So I made a conscious decision right there that I was going to rectify the situation. I was going to start work-ing harder. I was going to use my God-given ability. My whole attitude and personality changed that day. I decided to stop taking a secondary role. It was time to take charge of my own life, take charge of my destiny.

I'll give the coach credit, too. He took it all in stride. See, William Campbell was a little school, and most of the parents in town were factory workers or farmers. They had hard lives. One thing they loved to do was come out and watch their kids play sports. That was their release. I think the coach understood that. He didn't get mad. And he never talked to me about the incident. All I know is, I started practicing harder, and he started playing me more. Simple as that.

I made the varsity in tenth grade. Started both ways: linebacker on defense, tight end on offense. I still didn't like getting hit, but I learned how to deal with the fear. I became a pretty good football player. So did my brother Lawrence. He was the district's offensive player of the year; I was defensive player of the year. We both made all-state, things like that. But I had a lot of problems with the coaches and with some of the teachers. I've never been big on bowing down to authority, especially when I think the person in charge is an asshole. So I used to get suspended a fair amount. But it was so hypocritical. They'd start my suspension on a Thursday, let me come back the next day so that I could play in Friday night's game, then tell me to finish the suspension during the first part of the next week. What kind of message was that?

Going into my senior year I knew that I needed to keep my grades up so I could continue playing. So I tried to stay out of trouble. One day, though, I walked into a classroom and saw my brother Lawrence arguing with another student, a girl. They were dating at the time; unfortunately, Lawrence was also dating someone else. So now this girl was forcing a confrontation, and it was getting pretty ugly.

I had walked in right after the teacher, just a few seconds late for class. The rule in school was, if you were tardy three times, you got sent to the "pad room," where you had to sit quietly and just do work. The next step was suspension. This was my first tardy of the year, but all hell was breaking loose: kids screaming, the teacher trying to calm everyone down. The next thing I knew the teacher was taking all three of us to the principal's office. My brother and his girlfriend were both sent to the pad room; I ended up getting suspended. It always seemed as though if I was around when something bad was happening, I was going to get blamed. But they still wanted me to play football.

Don't get me wrong. I'm not saying I never did anything to warrant punishment. I don't mean to portray myself that way. When I was younger I skipped class and got in fights and did some things I shouldn't have done. I was always a cutup in the classroom, which pissed off a lot of teachers. But I always felt like my school gave me the shitty end of the stick. And not just me, but all poor kids. We were stereotyped. We were taught the way our parents were taught. By that I mean, if your parents went to college or your dad owned a store or something, then they'd put you in courses designed to prepare you for college. But if your parents were farmers or laborers or whatever, it was a whole different scenario. They'd put you in Future

Farmers of America and give you courses that made you feel like an idiot, because you were just going to end up shoveling pig shit on a farm or stuck in some lousy factory job anyway. So what was the point? I had one biology teacher, Mr. Rice, who was a fair man. Other than that, I didn't run across anyone who didn't stereotype me.

I had trouble with the football coaches, too, including the head coach, Ronald Cox, who was also the athletic director. The coaches wanted us to lift weights and work out during the summer. I understand that. It made sense. What they didn't understand was this: I had to survive. All the Haley kids worked like dogs in the summertime. We had to get jobs in order to buy clothes for the school year, because our parents couldn't afford to buy them for us. I had some shitty jobs, man. I used to pull tobacco every summer. The truck would come by and pick me up at 4:30 in the morning, and I'd lie in the back, trying to get a little more sleep on the way to the farm. Then I'd start working around 5:30 or 6:00, and the dew would still be on the plants and my hands would be freezing. But by 7:00 or 7:30, I'd be totally dry and burning up.

Pulling tobacco is tedious, debilitating work, even for a big, strong kid. The stalk is about five feet tall, and you start at the bottom of the plant, where it's yellow, and you reach around and pull up all the yellow leaves. Then you shove the leaves under your arms and go on to the next plant. You keep dropping your arms, stuffing the leaves there, trying to keep up with the tractor. You just keep moving and pulling, moving and pulling. Usually, everybody would get a row. And you'd do five rows at a time. Then the farmer would stop the tractor, and while everybody chucked the tobacco in, he'd go back and inspect the plants, because when people couldn't keep up, sometimes they'd skip a plant. If he discovered a plant that hadn't been pulled completely, he'd start cursing and yelling and bawling us out. Then he'd deduct money from the poor slob he caught.

Pulling tobacco was hard work, but not as hard as lifting pulp wood, which was brutal. We did that with our dad. He'd cut pine trees into five-and-a-half-foot lengths. Then we'd lift the wood on our shoulders and throw it on the back of a truck. After a few hours we were completely exhausted.

I don't mean to whine. The point is . . . we had to work. And if we weren't back from work in time to catch the activity bus, how were we supposed to get to school to lift weights and work out with the other kids on the team? Mom was working. Dad was working. Sometimes we'd walk or hitchhike, but shit, we lived twenty-five miles from school! You get tired of standing on the side of the road, hoping someone you know will drive on by and give you a lift. So I got penalized. I was told I wouldn't be eligible for any school awards my senior year. They let me play, and I made all-state, but I was at odds with the coaches all season.

I'm sure they didn't do anything to promote me. I never even knew what kind of opportunities were out there until after my senior year, when I got letters from Liberty Baptist and James Madison. And they're both Division I-AA schools. When I played in the Virginia All-Star Game at Virginia Tech, one of the coaches told some reporters that he thought I was a great athlete. That got me some attention, but by then it was too late. Almost everyone else who played in that game was being recruited by major Division I-A schools—places like the University of Virginia, Maryland, West Virginia. Not me. I was this scrawny kid, a 175-pound linebacker from little William Campbell High. No one had any idea who I was. For a kid to be properly recruited, his high school coaches have to give the college coaches an earful. That never happened with me. I was on my own. It was Liberty Baptist or James Madison. Or a lifetime in Gladys.

But I didn't mind. The fact that I had to work all through school put things in perspective for me. I know today that I'm a survivor. If need be, I can use my hands to make a living. Don't misunderstand me. I'm not happy that I had to grow up poor. I don't like the fact that we had to borrow water from neighbors and go to the bathroom in an outhouse, because we had no indoor plumbing until I was twelve years old, when we finally saved enough money to buy a double-wide mobile home. I hated it. Being poor sucked then, and it sucks now. But I'll tell you, 80 percent of the kids I knew were living like that.

My parents worked hard; they did their best. It just wasn't enough. That's why I always wanted to help them out—especially my mom. She had such a tough life—she deserved better. When she was a little girl she was hurt in a woodstove accident. Her arms were badly burned, and the doctors had to take skin grafts from her legs to repair the damage. That's one of the things I remember most about my mom. She would never wear short pants or short dresses, even in the summertime, when the heat was unbearable. Everything was below the knee, because she didn't want anyone to see the scars on her legs. But she never talked about it. She never complained.

When I was a little boy I used to have dreams about building a big new house for my mother. And it actually happened. That's one of the great things about being a professional athlete—you make enough money to take care of the people you love. My mom had spent her whole life in Gladys, and she wouldn't leave the neighborhood, so I bought some land and built a nice brick contemporary right across the street from where I grew up. She loves the house. There's only one problem: My father hasn't moved in. He stays across the street in his old house. See, my dad is a real prideful man. He doesn't like taking any kind of charity. I was just trying to help, of course, but maybe I didn't get enough input from him or something. Maybe I should have thought more about his feelings. I don't know. He tells me one day he's going to move, but he's just not ready yet. My parents still have a great relationship, though; in fact, it seems to be stronger than ever. That's cool. If they're happy, I'm happy.

The thing is, I was lucky. I had a talent that allowed me to get out of Gladys. But if a school doesn't give kids the opportunity to dream, then they'll be stuck living their parents' lives. Forever. That's one of the things that really pisses me off. My old school . . . they're always asking me to donate stuff, but I'm reluctant. I just can't get through all the hurt. Maybe it's different now, maybe they have better teachers. But I'm dealing with too much baggage. Usually I choose to work through my church back home. I donate to the church and hope they'll support the kids who dream. I believe they will. At the very least, I know that no one at church is going to say, "Oh, your daddy is just a lawnmower man, you don't need to get a good education." We *all* need it.

It's hard. The coaches and administrators at William Campbell send me stuff to autograph—sometimes I do it, sometimes I don't. My mom is on me about that. She says there are kids who would appreciate it. She's probably right. But I'll tell you: I don't want to be a role model. If they're looking for role models they need to look somewhere else, because I'm human. I make mistakes. And when somebody hurts me, I'm not receptive about giving back. People say, "You made it! Be happy! Now just shut up . . . and give!" It's not that simple. I'm not made that way.

CHAPTER 3

Big Man, Little Campus

The first time Danny Wilmer came to see me, I didn't know what to think. He was the offensive line coach at James Madison and he did most of the recruiting. At the time, I was more or less shocked that anyone wanted to offer me a scholarship, so I sat there quietly and listened. Coach Wilmer was a big guy, with a big head. He was kind of strange looking, but very impressive. And he could really talk. He motivated me. He made me want to play for him.

James Madison, located in Harrisonburg, Virginia, sounded like the perfect place: a small school, not too far away. I could make it there. Of course, no one outside my family had any faith in me. Toward the end of my senior year, I'd go into school and people would say, "Oh, you'll be back home in no time," or, "I'll give you a few weeks." And I would think, *Fuck you!* All that stuff I heard—from students, teachers, administrators, coaches, everybody—just made me more determined. They all thought I'd flunk out or get homesick or get in trouble; they assumed that something bad would happen and I'd come crawling back home. They just gave me another reason to stay at Madison: to prove them all wrong. They gave me the tools to go on and fight for what I wanted.

When I got to James Madison in the fall of 1982, Challace McMillin was the head coach. He was something else, a little man and a big-time Christian. He spoke in this soft voice, and he'd always sit real close to you, stare right into your eyes, maybe pat you on the arms or the legs. He was a strange little guy, and I never fully understood him, but he turned out to be something of a mentor to me. I used to do all kinds of crazy stuff during practice, like slamming people out of bounds, knocking them onto the track. I was violent, out of control. But Coach McMillin would get right on me and stay on me. He'd make me jog, do laps, and he'd bring me into his office all the time to talk. The thing about Coach McMillin was, he educated me about life; he didn't just use me as a football player. He was the first person to introduce me to mental imagery, which I use all the time now. I envision things, very clearly, unfolding exactly the way I want them to unfold. I know it's just a mind game, but it works.

Unfortunately, the other thing Coach introduced me to—and it fucks me up to this day—was this weird outlook on winning and losing. "Losing is not a reflection of you personally," he used to say. "It's just something that happens." To me, that's nothing more than a way to justify losing. I tried to turn him off on that shit. Other than that, though, I liked him a lot. He was a good man.

My roommate was a guy named James Harriston. He was another football player, a big defensive tackle (we called him "Big E") from Martinsville, Virginia. We hit it off right away, even though we were opposites. I was extreme, volatile; James was very laid-back, cool. He was a smart guy, too. In fact, he's a lawyer now. Classwork didn't give Big E a lot of trouble. But I had problems.

I went into college with a deficiency in reading and writing. I've worked at it for years, and I'm at the point now where I can sound the word out and get it down pretty much every time. Spelling still gives me trouble, though. That's one of the reasons I hate doing autograph sessions. There's nothing like sitting in a chair all day, trying to be friendly, and hearing someone say, "Dumb football player—he can't even spell my name right." That shit really gets on my nerves.

When I was a freshman in college, I couldn't afford to be too proud. I went to my first English class—English 101—and I knew right away that I needed help. The professor jumped right in and I didn't understand a whole lot of what she was talking about. Fortunately, Gary Clark was a junior at Madison at the time. Gary's a great guy (and a great football player—he had a fantastic career as a wide receiver with the Washington Redskins after he left James Madison), and he was more than happy to help me out. I went looking for him right after that first English class. Everything else I could handle. But I was worried about English. Gary told me the best place to go was the reading and writing lab. I didn't even know what it was, but I went there the next day.

The worst thing about reading and writing lab was that everyone knew why you were there. When other students saw you walk in that building, it was like there was a giant sign over the door: *Stupid people enter here.* I felt like I was going to special ed class in high school. I wanted to hide my face and sneak in. After a while, though, I just said, *The hell with it. This is going to help me.* If people wanted to think I was just a dumb jock, fine. They could think whatever the hell they wanted. After a few trips to lab, though, I discovered something: Athletes weren't the only ones who needed help. There were all kinds of kids in there: athletes and nonathletes, black, white, male, female. It was reassuring to know I wasn't alone.

The first semester I carried a C average—not great, but good enough to keep my scholarship and stay eligible for football. Within a year I stopped going to reading and writing lab, mainly because I had a great tutor and we usually worked somewhere else. She was incredibly smart, a straight-A student, and she was patient. We'd meet in a classroom, or outside, wherever I wanted to work. She was never condescending, never acted like I was wasting her time. She understood that we both had a job to do. Her job was to help me learn; my job was to give my best effort. I never expected her to do any work for me, and she didn't. She just helped me understand the material; the rest was up to me.

Of course, not all of my tutors were like that. Some were

good, some weren't so good. My attitude was, *If you're going to help me, then help me. But don't act like you're doing me any big favors. Remember, you're getting paid. Don't walk in with a big ego and start treating me like shit just because you have a 4.0 GPA and I have a 2.0. It doesn't mean you're better than me, any more than I'm better than you just because I play football.*

I went through a few tutors before I found the right one. Overall, though, my college experience was great. Unlike high school, my teachers at Madison really seemed to care. It's a small school, so you get to know just about everyone. And the professors were all willing to go out of their way to help. I don't mean they were trying to give us grades—they would never do anything like that. You had to work to earn your grades. But if you had a problem, and you really wanted to learn, they'd be there for you. That's one of the things I loved the most about Madison: it was personal. It was the kind of place where the president of the university would come into the cafeteria and eat dinner with you, just to make you feel at home.

Not that I ever felt out of place in the cafeteria. To me, the most incredible thing about college was the fact that you could get all the food you wanted. It was never like that at my house. We didn't starve or anything, but we were always hungry. Money was tight, and with five kids in the family, the dinner table could be a real battleground. So Madison was quite a change of pace. My first day there, during preseason practice, all these older guys were trying to cut in line in front of me at the cafeteria. There was some stupid protocol about freshmen stepping aside for upperclassmen. That shit wasn't going to happen to me. Pretty soon there was a little tussle, with the older players telling me what they were going to do to me out on the field that evening. I just said, "Bullshit! You're not getting in front of me. Get back in line." I guess they figured they were all bigger than me, older than me, they could do what they wanted. But it ain't the size of the dog in the fight, man. It's the fight that's in the dog. And this dog was *hungry*.

They got on me during practice, and they took their shots. But most of these guys were on offense, and when you're on offense, you have to worry about the ball. So I told them, "When that ball goes the other way, and you ain't looking at me, I'm gonna get you back, man." That's one of the reasons I love football: It's fair, in a perverse kind of way. *You want to hit me in the knees? Fine. Next play, I'm coming after your neck.*

That attitude led to my first encounter with a psychologist, a woman named Dr. Wallace. There was a perception among some of the coaches that I was having trouble . . . *adjusting.* So I was sent to Dr. Wallace. I talked to her about my feelings and she helped me relax. She was low-key, like she simply wanted to be my friend. That's cool. People have been forcing me to visit shrinks and psychologists all my life, and most of them have been crazier than me. But Dr. Wallace was all right. She got me to calm down a little bit.

There were no more fights at the cafeteria. Just a lot of eating. The first few weeks I would stand outside, waiting for the doors to open before each meal. Then I'd just sit in the back and eat, eat, eat. Two, three hours at a time. I'd eat until it hurt; until I couldn't move. Like a big old dog. It finally dawned on me after a few months that maybe I didn't have to sit in there all day, that no one was going to take the food away from me. But I wasn't alone. There were a lot of country boys at that school, and they all reacted the same way.

I was a starter my freshman year—inside linebacker, outside linebacker . . . wherever I was needed. James Madison is only Division I-AA. It had been admitting men for only twenty-five years, so there wasn't a long football history there. In other words, it wasn't exactly Notre Dame. But I'll tell you, man, it was exciting. To me, this was big-time college football. Of course, in a lot of ways I was just a clueless freshman. For example, we played one game at Virginia Military Institute. I'd never been there before, didn't know anything about it. Well, the first time VMI scored a touchdown, someone shot off a cannon. It's a tradition there—they do it after every touchdown. Most of the guys on the team knew all about it. No big deal. But it scared the hell out of me. I fell on the ground, put my hands over my ears, and started looking around for incoming aircraft. All of the young guys on the team—I think there were five us—just hit the ground. We were scared shitless. It's funny now, but I wasn't very amused at the time.

What was amusing was my first trip to Delaware State, which is a predominantly black university. As we drove up in our bus, they were marching out onto the football field to warm up. And we could hear their whole team chanting, "K-W-P! K-W-P!"

"What the hell does that mean?" I asked.

I forget who provided the answer, but it came quickly: "Kill the white people."

At the time, our team was half white, half black, so this made for a fairly amusing situation. The white guys were scared, I could tell. But the black guys were eating it up, saying, "Hmmm, they ain't mad at me, man. They're mad at you. They'll probably leave the brothers alone, but they're gonna *kill* y'all!" I'd never seen some of these guys so nervous. It was tense for a few minutes, until the last of the Delaware State players marched past the bus, and at the end of the line were these two little white guys, with big, floppy helmets and ill-fitting shoulder pads . . . and they were chanting, too! Two itty-bitty white guys, clapping their hands, marching along, shouting, "K-W-P! K-W-P!"

Fucking hysterical. The whole bus just fell apart, laughing. Maybe that was their plan: to immobilize us with humor. If so, it worked, because they kicked our asses that day.

———————

I have very few complaints about my time at Madison. I had a wonderful football career—never missed a game, led the team in tackles in each of my last three seasons, earned Division I-AA All-America honors as a senior. I'm even a member of the JMU Hall of Fame, which makes me really proud. Best of all, I met my wife, Karen, while I was there. When I first arrived she was dating another guy on the team, a senior. So I didn't talk to her much the first couple years. When I was a junior, though, she was available, so me and my best friend, Warren Marshall, made a little bet on who could get a date with her first. She used to work at the front desk of the student union. She was really pretty and smart, and I don't think she took me seriously, at first. But I did all kinds of crazy stuff to get her attention. I'd send her flowers, write poetry, call her up all the time. Eventually she gave in and we went out on a date —to McDonald's, I think—and I won the bet. And then I fell in love with her.

Karen has some very strong, and not particularly kind, opinions about college athletes. She generally thinks they get a free ride. She was an exceptional student—she has a master's in political science from James Madison, and she taught there, too. She worked her way through college, paid every penny with the help of the ROTC program. One thing that drives her nuts is seeing athletes who just skate along. That bothers me, too. I was fortunate. When Madison recruited me, the thing they told my mom was, "He'll get an education first, he'll play football second." And they meant it. I graduated right on time, with a degree in sociology. I'm proud of that accomplishment, although at the time it didn't seem like such a big deal, since it was what was expected of me—and every other athlete at Madison.

Today, though, it's incredibly rare to see a kid come into the NFL with a degree in hand. Most of the guys I see aren't even close. They have a handful of credits from courses that have no connection to each other. A lot of them would have to go back to school for four more years to have any hope of getting a degree. And yet, somehow, they kept playing football. They maintained their eligibility. The hypocrisy makes me want to puke.

But I understand it. Even at Madison, where education was valued, there was a premium placed on winning. I don't care where you coach—Duke, Princeton, Harvard—you don't keep your job by keeping kids in school. Challace McMillin had one of the highest graduation rates around, but they eventually forced him out, because ultimately it's the W's and L's that count. We won nine games and lost thirteen in Coach McMillin's last two years, and that just wasn't good enough. It's all about politics, even at a place like Madison. They want to win games so they can move up in the rankings, which puts more people in the stands, which leads to bigger contributions from the alumni and more applications, and more money for the school. Simple as that. It's like Reaganomics: Everything trickles down.

You see, it's all about the money. College presidents talk about wanting student-athletes to graduate, but what they really want is to win. And if someone has to suffer, then let it be the kids. Because if the kid doesn't suffer—if you put him first and force him to get an education, to go to class, to take his tests, and to pass his tests—then the football team and basketball team are going to suffer. And if the teams suffer, the school suffers.

Sick, huh? But it's the truth, especially at the major univer-

sities, the ones with the football factories. What I see today
are a lot of universities making piles of money on the backs of
these kids—and not doing anything to help them in return.
Yeah, I know, they're giving the kids scholarships, but that's
not enough. Not when you're spending thirty hours a week
practicing and playing football, and you're too tired to get up
for class and you can't put a dime in your pocket because the
NCAA won't even let you hold down a part-time job. Coaches
get six-figure shoe deals, universities get millions from the television networks and bowl sponsors. What do the kids get?
Fucked, that's what they get. Most of them are poor. Why not
give them an allowance as compensation for generating so
much revenue? It would have to be monitored, obviously, but
at least it would give kids a chance to stay clean. They'd be
less likely to get locked up by agents, or to take money from
boosters. And there has to be more accountability. If you're
going to accept a kid into school, and then chew him up on
the football field, you at least have an obligation to see to it
that he does everything possible to get a degree. Because I'm
telling you, 98 percent of these kids are never going to make
it in the NFL. And right now, no one gives a shit—not the universities, not the league, not the coaches. And certainly not the
fans. The schools and the NCAA talk about stricter guidelines,
but their wallets keep getting fatter and fatter. Seems pretty
hypocritical to me.

But what's the answer? Do you make higher education
available only to a privileged few? I don't think so. I think that
Proposition 48—which mandated that athletes had to meet

certain academic requirements in order to compete as freshmen—was a mistake to begin with. If you keep raising standards, you cut off a certain segment of the population—mostly minority kids from poor families. And a lot of those kids would succeed in college if you gave them a chance. But the NBA, NFL, and the NCAA have to get together and come up with some kind of agreement. If a kid signs with a college and then after a year he wants to go to the NFL, maybe the NFL should say no. Maybe there should be a minimum age requirement. There has to be some way to keep kids in school, to make sure they get an education. Because most of them will fail as athletes.

I see kids get cut now and they're just fucking devastated. They sit around for a full year, working out a little, talking about trying again. Then they get cut again. In the meantime, what have they done to prepare for the future? Nothing. I tell them to get a job, even if it's only temporary, because they can always quit the job later, if they hook up with a team. Or go back to school. Do *something!*

But they don't. Every so often you see someone like Emmitt Smith, a player who returns to school and completes his degree—even though he doesn't have to. That shows character, and I admire him for it. But most guys just quit, especially the ones who need the degree most. Pretty soon they start falling behind on payments and stuff. They get in trouble, and then their hands are out, looking for help. I'm a sucker for that stuff. But I have a motto: *You can come to the well once. It dries up fast.*

Part of the problem is that some kids don't want to be in college and don't belong in college. It would be nice if there were developmental leagues for kids like that, to help them prepare specifically for careers in professional sports. That'll never happen, though, because the only people who stand to benefit are the kids themselves. The colleges would be hurt because they'd lose so much talent. And the NFL and NBA would never go for it because they like having established stars coming into their leagues. The NCAA *is* their developmental league—and it's free! Why would they fund their own?

When I talk to elementary school kids or high school kids, I tell them to look for a small school where they can get an education and play football for four years. If you're good enough, the NFL will find you. And when you get there, you'll have growing power. You'll have a chance to improve, which is something I rarely see among the top-notch Division I guys. They come into the NFL, and they're as good as they're gonna get. But the guys who come from smaller schools seem to grow. They get better and better. And they're smarter.

I'm living proof.

CHAPTER 4

Why George Seifert Can't Carry Bill Walsh's Clipboard

When I came into the NFL in 1986, I wasn't in awe of anyone. I had been drafted by the San Francisco 49ers in the fourth round, and it never occurred to me to that I might not get a lot of playing time right away. I was going to one of the most successful, competitive franchises in professional football, but I didn't even know it. In college, just like in high school, I was a player, not a spectator or a fan. I didn't know who Joe Montana was, I didn't know who Ronnie Lott was. Hell, I didn't even know who Bill Walsh was. I had no idea who I was supposed to respect or not respect. Maybe that worked in my favor. I tell kids today: The worst thing you can do is go in there in awe of anyone, especially if it's somebody whose damn job you want to take someday. I'm not saying you should be a rookie asshole; but in your heart, you have to believe you're an equal.

When I became an established NFL player, I was always willing to help out younger guys, show them the ropes. My attitude was, *Go ahead, bring in a first-round draft pick and let him try to take my job. I'll teach him everything I know, and he still won't be able to do it.* I figured the competition was healthy, and in the end, maybe the younger guy would learn something. But a lot of guys are not like that. They're scared. So they'll take a young kid and pretend to help him, give him the big shoulder to lean on. Then they'll give him the wrong directions, and the kid fucks up in practice, and . . . *Bam!* He's gone. Problem solved. Because once they label you as stupid, your ass is on the back burner. So my advice is this: Don't listen to anybody except the coaches. And half the time don't even listen to them, because they don't know what the hell they're talking about either. Just get your ass up into your room, study your playbook, memorize it, do your fucking homework! Make it impossible for them not to notice you.

That's what I did my rookie year. I studied harder than everyone else. I knew the whole playbook—everything. I knew what I was supposed to do, I knew what all of the linebackers were supposed to do. I knew what the defensive linemen were supposed to do. I knew more than they thought I needed to know.

Knowledge was power. I could see that the first time I met Bill Walsh, the 49ers head coach. He was very laid-back, but very confident, very smart. He never gave his mind a rest; he was always thinking, always two steps ahead of everyone else. My first year, during mini-camp, he gave this broad speech to all the rookies, explaining what was required of each player.

He was so articulate, so charismatic, that you felt compelled to listen. He wasn't a rah-rah kind of guy, but he'd fill you up. He'd make you want to work for him. That spring, when I was still a senior at James Madison, he told me to go back to school, finish my degree, and show up in the summer ready to play football. I couldn't wait to get back, even though I was nervous about being so far from home.

The 49ers were planning on using me at both defensive end and linebacker, so I worked out that whole summer with Tommy Hart, the defensive line coach. Tommy was a hell of a player in his day—spent thirteen years in the NFL (including ten with the 49ers) in the 1960s and '70s—and he's one of the best coaches I've ever worked with. He tested me: mentally as well as physically. He used to make me stay out on the field for two or three hours working on pass rushing. And this was usually after I had worked out with the strength and conditioning coach. That whole summer I was just exhausted.

One of the first days in camp Tommy was trying to teach me a particular technique. He'd snap the ball and then tell me to hit him, like he was an offensive lineman. I was up to 225 pounds by this time. I was in great shape. So I was thinking, *Shit, I'll hurt this old man if I hit him.* But he kept snapping the ball and I kept screwing up, going half-speed, and finally he just stopped and looked at me, kind of disgusted.

"Get over there and play offense. I'll show you how it's done."

I shrugged. *This ought to be good.*

I had my shoulder pads and helmet on. Tommy was wearing a T-shirt and shorts. He came off the ball and he slapped my shoulder and I just went flying. I mean, it was unbelievable! This old man—he was forty-two—just whacked me halfway across the field, like I was a little kid. From that day on I had total respect for that man. I took my game to a new level of intensity. All I needed was a water break once in a while.

———

My first two years in San Francisco were productive. By any objective standard, I guess you'd have to say I was progressing nicely. I had twelve sacks in '86—a club record for a rookie; in '86 and '87 I was the team leader in sacks. My personal life was healthy, too. Karen and I were married in 1987, after my rookie season. We had a big church wedding in Richmond, Virginia, Karen's hometown. A lot of my friends and coaches from James Madison showed up. A few of my new 49ers teammates, too. It was a nice ceremony.

All in all, life was pretty good. I had a new wife, a great job, a good paycheck.

But I wasn't content. I was getting lots of playing time, mostly at what we called the "elephant" position—which was like a combination linebacker/defensive end specializing in pass rushing. But I wasn't starting. Milt McColl would usually start, play the first two plays, then I'd come in for the rest of the game. That really bothered me. I wanted to be a starter. I wanted the money and the respect that comes with being a starter. I had earned it. I *deserved* it. But it seemed like I was the only person who felt that way.

Prior to the 1988 season, though, Bill Walsh summoned me

to his office. I was nervous. There was a lot of shit going on at the time. I was trying to redo my contract, and there were some bad feelings about that. John McVay, the general manager, had no interest in renegotiating, and I felt like the suits in the front office didn't appreciate my contributions. So it got kind of ugly for a while. When the word came down that Bill wanted to meet with me, I presumed something horrible was about to happen. I thought he was going to trade me or release me. Just brush me aside. But it wasn't like that at all.

I walked into his office and looked around. I'd never been in there before. It was very large, very intimidating. Bill closed the door and asked me to sit down. We made small talk for a while. He asked me how everything was going; he asked about my wife. I told him I was trying to buy a house in San Francisco, but that it was extremely expensive (a little hint there). Finally there was a break in the conversation and Bill just stared at me. Then he leaned forward.

"Charles, do you think you can handle a starting job?"

I was floored. Here I thought I was about to be released, and instead the guy was giving me a promotion.

"Yes, sir," I said, because I couldn't think of anything else to say.

He smiled. "Well, then . . . you're the starter. From now on, the job is yours to lose."

I swear . . . I wanted to jump up and give the man a hug. It was all I ever wanted—someone to give me an opportunity and then set the standard. That was one of the happiest days of my life. It gave me new hope, because I had been on the verge of shutting down. You get no respect or recognition for your work when you're playing behind someone—no matter how well you play. The starter gets the recognition, the rewards. And now I was a starter.

Our chemistry was great that season. Several of the guys who had come in my rookie year became starters. We had a nice mix of youth and experience. We had Joe Montana, the Magic Man, at quarterback. We had Jerry Rice and John Taylor at receiver. We had Roger Craig in the backfield. We had me and Ronnie Lott, maybe the best safety who's ever played the game, leading the defense. And, of course, we had the genius: Bill Walsh.

As a rule, I don't listen to pregame speeches. I've heard a lot of them over the years, and they're usually just some bullshit ranting and raving. I don't need that. So I tune it out. But it was different with Bill. He didn't bother with cheerleading. Instead, he'd be very calm. He'd go over the game plan and say, "This is what we have to do. We have to go out and block and tackle and execute. These are not monsters we're facing. They are men . . . football players. Just like you."

We beat the Cincinnati Bengals in Super Bowl XXIII that year. In the days leading up to the game there was a lot of publicity about it being some sort of personal confrontation between Bill and Sam Wyche, the Bengals coach. Wyche had been an assistant for the 49ers in 1982; Bill had given him his first job in the pros. So there was a lot of emotion surrounding the game. When we were in the locker room, though, getting ready to go out on the field, Bill knew exactly what to say: "This isn't a game between Sam Wyche and Bill Walsh. This is a game between the Cincinnati Bengals and the San Francisco 49ers. We're just the coaches. You have to play the game." As usual, he broke everything down into fine print. There was no shouting, no hysterics. Just business. It was always that way with Bill, no matter how important a game it was. I enjoyed listening to him and I enjoyed playing for him, because you could actually learn something. Spitting, yelling, cussing people out —that doesn't work for most players. It just makes them more uptight, especially right before a game. Bill was like the coaches I had in college: smart, methodical; he took the time to explain everything.

Sometimes he didn't even need much time. I remember one practice session in which he really separated himself from every other coach I'd ever seen—and every coach I've seen since. The defense was shutting down the offense, just jamming them on every play. Most coaches would have just let it go on and said, "We'll review the film and handle it later." Not Bill. He blew his whistle, stopped practice, and sent someone in to get a clipboard. He scribbled on the thing for about five minutes while we all stood there picking our noses, wondering what the hell was going on. Then all of a sudden he stopped.

"Joe!" he yelled. "Come over here. And bring the offense with you."

So Montana walked over, dragging the whole offensive team with him. They formed a little circle around Bill, and I could see him pointing and talking, and then the guys began nodding, as if they understood something. A few minutes later they started kicking our asses. Just like that. Bill figured it out. That's the way he worked. He took advantage of the moment.

But Bill was more than just a good coach. He was a good man who truly cared about his players. For example, he introduced a program designed to help players who hadn't received their college degrees. If a guy wanted to go back to school and complete his education, the team would pick up 50 percent of the tab. He brought in financial advisors to help people invest their money wisely. More than once I saw guys fuck up and Bill would bail them out, one way or another. He believed in helping players. He wanted his men, when they finished playing, to have some money in their pockets. And he didn't mind talking about that stuff. He also believed in recruiting minority coaches, giving them opportunities. I'm not talking about quotas. I'm talking about giving qualified minorities a fair shot. Bill would bring young minority coaches into training camp and give them a chance to learn the system, so that maybe someday they could become NFL head coaches. He didn't put people in there just for the sake of appearance; he opened the door and told them to apply themselves. Yes, Bill was a good football coach. He did all the things a coach is supposed to do. But he also took the time to find out about the other side of a player's life. He saw the big picture. That made me have a ton of respect for him.

Unfortunately, right after we won the Super Bowl, Bill announced his retirement. I couldn't believe it. We were world champions; I had just been named to the Pro Bowl for the first time. But I was so sad I didn't even feel like celebrating. No one had ever shown so much faith in me—as a person and a player. And now he was leaving. I wondered what would become of the 49ers. I wondered what poor sucker was going to have to try to fill Bill Walsh's shoes.

We didn't have to wait long for an answer. Within a few days George Seifert was promoted to head coach. George was the 49ers defensive coordinator. To be perfectly honest, I thought he was one of the best defensive coordinators I'd ever been around. He knew his shit. But he had a lousy personality. He just didn't know how to communicate with people—especially black people. I first discovered this in my rookie year, when we did a charity event at Great America, a theme park located near the 49ers' training facility. At one point he was standing with his family, and he said, "Charles, I want to introduce you to my wife." So I walked over, put out my hand, and Seifert said, "Honey, this is Charles Haley. You know what? I can't believe it. He didn't make a single mistake in practice today! Isn't that something?"

I was furious. I'd been working my ass off in practice, studying film every day, memorizing the playbook, and he was acting like I was some kind of idiot. To me, he might as well have said, *I can't believe a black guy could play like that, because you know how stupid those black players are. They always make mistakes.* I don't know if that comment reflected the way he really felt, but I saw things over the next few years that led me to believe it probably did. It was open to interpretation, and I know how I interpreted it at the time. But I was a rookie, so I just put it in the back of my mind. I filed it away in a little compartment marked *Asshole*! I didn't smile, I didn't frown, I didn't say anything. But I never forgot it.

To the casual observer, it probably looked like the 49ers made a smooth transition from Bill Walsh to George Seifert in 1989. After all, we kicked ass all year: 14–2 in the regular season, two easy victories in the NFC playoffs. In January there we were again, back in the Super Bowl, and this time it wasn't even a contest. We hammered the Denver Broncos 55–10 in the most lopsided Super Bowl ever played. I had another good season personally, too: started every game, led the team in sacks . . . even scored my first touchdown.

But you know what? It wasn't nearly as satisfying as the previous season. Yeah, we kept on winning, but it was all Bill's stuff that allowed us to win. It was Bill's team, Bill's system, and it would take a couple years for Seifert to fuck it up completely. He did enough wrong that first year to make it pretty miserable, though. Practices got longer and more disorganized. There was less communication between players and coaches. George's main problem was that he wanted to prove to everyone that he was just as smart as Bill, that he could be a guru, too. He was a very impressive defensive coordinator, but all of a sudden he wanted to run the offense, too. And the team suffered.

We did a steady slide over the next two years. The Giants beat us in the NFC title game after the 1990 season, and in 1991 we didn't even make the playoffs. I had a couple of good seasons—great, actually: I was named NFC Defensive Player of the Year in 1990 and made the Pro Bowl in both '90 and '91—but I didn't have a lot of fun. I had lost respect for Seifert as a coach; worse, I had lost whatever little respect I had for him as a man.

When I was in San Francisco, Seifert's way of dealing with black players was to bring in Harry Edwards. Dr. Edwards is a professor of sociology at Cal-Berkeley. He used to be a radical, but now I think he's all about the money. Give him a check and he'll help your team solve its racial problems. It was kind of pathetic, really. He'd come around, acting like he belonged, telling stories about how he used to be with the Black Panthers and shit. Most guys would just try to ignore him. We all knew why he was there: to be the mediator between the coaching staff and the black players. It was like Seifert said, *"I'll handle the white guys, you talk to the black guys."* What kind of bullshit is that?

Dr. Edwards was supposed to help the 49ers achieve racial harmony. If a problem came up, he was asked to deal with it. For example, let's say some guys were talking about interracial marriage. That kind of stuff happens in a locker room. You know, we bust each other's balls all the time. If a black guy was going to marry a white girl, we might say, "Damn, man, why you want to do that? You have any idea how hard it's gonna be?" Dr. Edwards would hear something like that and walk over and kind of whisper in your ear: "Come on now, we don't need to be talking like that?" Well, yeah, we *do* need to be talking like that. Because at least if we're talking, maybe we're educating each other a little bit. And anyway, this was stuff that was coming from within—it was locker room stuff; it was team stuff. Edwards was an outsider. Instead of helping, his presence just created a bigger divide between the black players and the white players.

Most of the black players I know disliked Dr. Edwards, because it was pretty obvious that he'd sold out a long time ago. He wasn't concerned with the welfare of the black player; he was concerned with his own paycheck. To be fair, I have to admit that it wasn't Seifert's idea to bring in Edwards—it was Bill Walsh's idea. But he didn't really have a role under Bill. He'd just come in once in a while, talk to a few players, and then be gone. We didn't see him that much. Under Seifert, Edwards's role expanded. He would tell the front office who they should draft, who they shouldn't draft. It was like they thought that Dr. Edwards, just because he was black, would be able to look at a player and say, *"Well, he's from Watts, so he'll have this problem or that problem."* That's bullshit, of course, and I told them so: Edwards and Seifert. But Edwards kept hanging around, trying to talk to me. I swear, there were times when it seemed like he was brought in specifically to tame me. But he never did.

Seifert tried to work some other nonsense on me, too. I found out later—after I left the team—that he had told Tim Harris to start a fight with me, to make me look bad. The 49ers brought in Tim in '91. He was a good football player

. . . and a big talker, just like me. So we'd talk shit to each other all the time—on the field, in the locker room. Next thing I knew, the newspapers were printing stories about the 49ers shopping me around. Supposedly, there was this big battle between me and Tim; he was going to take my starting job and I was so angry about it that I was becoming a distraction to the team.

What the newspapers didn't know was that Tim and I were pretty good friends. We were competitive, but we respected each other. After work we'd get together and kick it, have a few beers, laugh about the whole thing. There was one incident involving me and Tim that was wildly misinterpreted. It happened during my last week with the 49ers, when I was about ready to kill George Seifert. I was drinking at a Bennigan's across the street from the 49ers' practice facility, and after a while I got it into my head that I wanted to confront that motherfucker. So I went looking for him. By the time I got to Seifert's office, though, he was gone. I walked out into the parking lot and realized that I had to take a piss. But I didn't want to go back inside to use the bathroom. So I took a leak on the ground next to my car. Unfortunately, I was parked right next to Tim Harris's car. And Tim walked out just as I was doing my business.

"Hey, you better not pee on my car, man."

"Don't worry about it."

Tim knew I was drunk and he was just messing around with me. Unfortunately, a security guard heard Tim talking to me and got it into his head that we were having some kind of a fight . . . and that I really was pissing on the man's car. Pretty soon the newspapers got to the security guard and it became a huge fucking story. And it was *all wrong!* A few years later, at a retirement banquet for Joe Montana, Tim told me about Seifert encouraging him to start a fight with me. Didn't work, though. Fucking Seifert . . . the man didn't even know his own players. Me and Tim used to close bars, man. When I get to California, we still go out and kick it. You think he was going to take a pop at me? The only thing we ever argued about was who was going to have the most sacks.

The 49ers did a lot of things like that my last couple years. They tried to get at me. But they couldn't. I wouldn't let them. Before the start of the '91 season Seifert was calling me into his office every day, giving me a lecture. Every fucking day, man! I had to go in there and listen to him tell me what I should talk about and what I shouldn't talk about; how to talk to coaches, teammates, the media. Here I was, fresh off my best season as a pro—NFC Defensive Player of the Year!— and they were treating me like dirt. I was like, *God damn! When Bill was here he didn't have any trouble with me. All of a sudden I'm the biggest problem on this team? How the hell did that happen?*

As far as I could tell, the problem was George Seifert and some of the front office personnel. They're the ones who decided to release a bunch of the guys who had led us to two straight Super Bowls: Keena Turner left in 1990, and Ronnie Lott, Matt Millen, and Roger Craig were lost through free agency in '91. I mean, I know times change and you have to make adjustments. But we had a dynasty, and they released a lot of people who could have passed on their knowledge, maybe kept the tradition alive. But no . . . instead, the burden immediately went from their shoulders to my shoulders. And when I tried to talk about it, those motherfuckers started ordering me to see a shrink every other damn week. I sat next to Michael Carter, the 49ers nose tackle, in the locker room. I'm telling you, from the day I walked in until the day I left, he never said a damn word to anybody. But when I didn't feel like talking, they thought there was something wrong with me and they'd make me go see a psychiatrist. Then when I did start talking, they'd tell me to shut up. It was like a campaign or something.

My frustration reached a peak in the fifth week of the '91 season, when we lost to the Los Angeles Raiders, Ronnie Lott's new team. After the game I had a slight nervous breakdown—or whatever you want to call it. Basically I lost control and gave the 49ers reason to believe that I really was crazy. It just seemed like I was the only guy out there playing hard, and I went up to George and told him, "You know, you've got to start coming down on these guys." Everybody had big contracts, everybody was fat, with full pockets. They weren't playing hard anymore. They weren't hungry. But when you try to point out something like that, when you try to express your opinion, coaches always think, *You're a dumb-ass football player and you can't tell me anything.*

I tried, though. Man, did I try. When the game ended those motherfuckers came in, and I really gave it to them. I started cussing out the whole team. George got sick of listening to me, I guess, so he grabbed my arm, and when he did that I just lost it. I took a swing right at his smug little head. Fortunately, I missed. But I did hit the wall, and it hurt so much—left a big knuckle print—that I got even more pissed off. I started bouncing around, cursing, yelling, throwing shit. Then I put my hand through a window and cut it to pieces. They had to stitch me up in the locker room.

I don't know what I was thinking. My temper had gotten me in trouble before, but this was like nothing I'd ever experienced. I was in a complete fucking rage. Some of the other players tried to hold me down after a while, but I wouldn't let them. Finally, they tracked down Ronnie in the other locker room, and he came running in. I remember he was half-naked —shorts, no shirt, no shoes. He sat down next to me, held my hand, and kept telling me everything would be all right. I just sat there shaking, crying. It was so emotional. I can't really explain what happened, except to say that I felt like they were trying to destroy me . . . and they almost succeeded.

The next day I was back to my old self. Just for laughs I came to work in a camouflage outfit that my wife had given me. That raised a few eyebrows: have a nervous breakdown on Sunday and show up Monday dressed like a fucking commando. I was just messing around with them, but you should have seen the looks I got. Talk about people scattering. Players were diving headfirst into the meeting rooms. I told the trainer that I had a headache, and he sent me home right away. I'm pretty sure they thought I was going to hurt somebody.

Dr. Edwards obviously did. I later heard he went around telling all the black guys, "This motherfucker is crazy! And if he doesn't get some psychiatric help, then we don't want him playing." I'll be the first to admit that I have trouble controlling my anger. But I've always worked hard, and I've always been true to my word, which is a lot more than most people can say. I gave the 49ers everything I had. Was I the perfect little soldier? No. I'm not big on conformity. Never have been, never will be. If you want Charles Haley on your football team, you get the whole package: body, mind, mouth. Obviously, the 49ers no longer wanted this package, and I wanted no part of the 49ers. They were trying to take away my credibility with the other players, which was just about the worst thing they could have done. So I spent the rest of the season trying to get under their skin. If they were going to fuck with me, I was going to fuck with them.

By the summer of 1992 we were heading for a divorce, me and the 49ers. There were a couple of incidents that brought the whole situation to a head, one of which involved Harry Edwards. I was in the weight room, working out, when he confronted me.

"Charles, come here. I want to talk to you."

"I don't want to hear your shit," I said, and the next thing I knew he was in my face. He said some things, I said some things. It wasn't a pleasant conversation. Nevertheless, I had no intention of letting it get physical. Edwards is six-nine, 300 pounds, and I was sure he could take care of himself. But he was also an old man. If I took a swing at him, my career was over. Unfortunately, he took a swing at *me*. I had two choices: fight back and maybe end up in jail, or try to get out of there. I chose the second option. I started backpedaling out of the room while he was throwing punches. Pretty soon we were out in the hallway and it was over. His arms got tired, I guess. He kept yelling at me, but I just walked away.

To this day I believe the thing that bothered Edwards the most was the fact that I had more respect from the players than he did. It was about control. The guys listened to me more than they listened to him. And his job was dependent on getting the players to listen. I got in his way, and he didn't like it.

Most of the problems I've had in my professional career stem from the fact that I don't just bow to authority. I believe in doing things my own way. The NFL is a rigid place. I'm not a real rigid guy. I will not blindly follow someone I do not respect, even if that person determines my playing time or signs my paycheck. Unfortunately, expressing your opinion in the NFL can get you in trouble. (This was true in San Francisco, and it's especially true in Dallas, where a Cowboy can't take a piss without reading about it in the newspaper the next day.) The sad truth is, it's hard to be an individual in professional sports. The system generally rewards those who conform and punishes those who rebel. I was a rebel, no question about it. And George Seifert didn't want any rebels on his team, no matter how well they could play.

I spent most of training camp just waiting for the ax to fall.

They weren't going to cut me, of course—that would have been stupid. But the situation was pretty much unmanageable. I wanted out and they wanted me out. Seifert was pissed off because I had refused to make an overseas trip with the team. Instead, I told him I was going to stay behind and get my knee worked on, which was exactly what I did (I had to have some torn cartilage removed). At the same time, I was trying to re-work my contract, so there was a lot of tension about that. I was working out mostly on my own, rather than with the team.

On August 26, just a week before the season was to begin, I got a call from Bill McPherson, the defensive coordinator. Bill said that George was very upset, that he'd never had a player talk to him the way I had, and that he wasn't going to put up with it any longer. He and the front office people—Carmen Policy, the president; Dwight Clark, the new coordinator of football operations (and a former 49ers wide receiver); even Eddie DeBartolo, the owner—were discussing trade options. But Coach Mac wanted me to stay, so he asked me to go to Seifert's office and talk to him. I think he wanted me to apologize, try to smooth things over. There was no way that was going to happen, but I said I'd stop by.

I went up to Seifert's office the next morning. That bitch was so nervous it was almost comical. He kept moving around, sitting in every chair in the room, twitching, stuttering. I barely talked at all. I was torn between leaving peacefully and breaking my foot off in his ass. I decided to listen, because there was a time when I had a ton of respect for the man.

"You're a hell of a football player, Charles," he said. "But some of the things that have happened . . . we just can't have it anymore. We can't have you bad-mouthing players and coaches. So we're trying to work a deal for you."

A few hours later they told me I had been traded to the Cowboys. I was a bargain, as it turned out. The 49ers were so eager to get rid of me that they demanded nothing more than a pair of draft picks. I walked out of camp that day feeling almost tranquil. I had made a decision to be quiet about the whole matter, just move on and start over. I wanted to keep it cool. But right away those assholes started blasting me—players, coaches, administration. Before I even arrived in Dallas there was a newspaper story in which Carmen Policy said, "I'd call it an attitude problem. Dallas is getting a good player. But sometimes Charles's personality was so divergent from the team that he became a distraction. Let's just say it's in our best interest to have him playing elsewhere. "

Okay, fine. I had made my own bed. I had clashed with the front office, and they'd gotten rid of me. I had too many enemies in powerful positions. Seifert couldn't have a player on his team who wouldn't do exactly what he was told; Dwight was new on the job and he wanted to get rid of a lot of the older players so he could be the man and no one would bad-mouth him. I still think Carmen got suckered. He was fed a lot of bad information and he got caught in the middle. But it's like this: When you make a trade, you have to justify it. What are you going to say: "Charles is a hell of a guy and a great player, but we traded him anyway"? I don't think so. I still like Carmen. What he said was in the heat of battle. He was good to my family, so I'll cut him some slack. The same is true of Eddie DeBartolo. I have nothing but admiration for Eddie D. I think he'll go down as one of the greatest owners in NFL history.

Even George . . . When I left, I wasn't that angry with him anymore. If people hadn't come to me later, I wouldn't have known about some of the underhanded shit he tried to pull, like with Tim Harris. The thing is, a lot of players will do dirt for a coach; they'll do anything to save their jobs. But sooner or later, their conscience hits their ass, and they have to talk about it. It's their way of justifying it. Afterward, they feel better.

But it just makes me hate a little bit more.

Charles in Charge, Part II
"YOU CAN GO NOW, MR. HALEY"

There's a very fine line between fantasy and reality. If you know how to walk that line, you can use it to your advantage.

In my first year in the NFL the 49ers introduced a program incorporating mandatory drug testing and psychological counseling for all rookies. The league had nothing to do with this. It was strictly in-house—Bill Walsh's idea, and I'm sure he had the players' best interests at heart. But, man, I hated that program. Made me feel like a criminal. And a crazy criminal at that. There's nothing worse than having a shrink ask you all sorts of personal questions when you don't even want to be there.

The woman who ran the program was actually very nice. I don't remember her name, but we used to have to go to the Holiday Inn to meet her once a week. We'd spend thirty minutes talking to her, and then we had to provide a urine sample. Nice combination, huh? The first time was pretty basic and boring. She talked to me, said we were going to get into my family history and stuff. When I was a rookie I didn't talk much, and that made some people nervous. I was just watching and learning. That's the way I am. I figured I'd start opening up a little when I got comfortable. But I guess the 49ers had a different agenda for my ass. So this psychologist fired a bunch of questions at me and I answered maybe one or two. Then she gave up, handed me a cup, and sent me into the bathroom to take a piss. She did that all day, with maybe a dozen different players.

I decided before I left that I wasn't going to go through even one more week of this nonsense. But I couldn't just refuse to show up. They'd fine me or suspend me if I tried that. No . . . I needed a plan.

The next week I stopped at a bar and had a few drinks right before my appointment. I was putting my game face on. By the time I walked into her office, I was ready.

"How are you doing," she said.

"Not too good."

I fell onto the couch and let out a heavy sigh. She seemed concerned. Before long we were talking about my whole life, and I was giving her some pretty juicy details. Not true details, but definitely juicy. I told her I came from an abusive family, that my father used to beat the crap out of me every day. I started crying, weeping uncontrollably, sobbing and moaning. Eventually the subject turned to sex, just like I figured it would.

"Tell me about your first sexual encounter."

So I did. I told her what it was like to grow up in the rural South, where men are men and farm animals are scared. I told her about the day I lost my virginity to a neighbor's sheep. And then all of a sudden I stopped talking and jumped off the couch and screamed at the top of my lungs. Not words, just noise; the sounds of a lunatic.

"Aaaahhhhhh!"

The poor woman fell over backward in her chair. Right onto the floor. Scared half to death, she scrambled to her feet and tried to brush the wrinkles out of her suit. She pointed toward the bathroom.

"J-j-just go in there," she stammered, pointing toward the bathroom. "Leave a sample, and then you can go."

"We're done?" I asked, trying to sound like I was disappointed.

"Yes," she said. "We're done. You don't have to come back anymore."

And that's the way it was. The other rookies kept going, but not me. It wasn't long before word came down that I was crazy, that I had a few screws loose. I didn't care. In fact, I kind of liked it. I still do. If people don't know whether you're pulling their chain or being real, you have an edge. And in the fucked-up world of professional football, every little advantage helps.

CHAPTER 5

Why Steve Young Can't Carry Joe Montana's Jockstrap

It isn't easy being a rookie in the National Football League. You're in a new city, playing with new teammates, trying to learn a new system, fighting for a job. And no one really cares whether you make it or not. I was lucky. A few people took the time to help me out, to make my life a little easier. One of them was Joe Montana.

Like I said, when I arrived in San Francisco I was basically clueless. Most of the other rookies had been big-time football fans their entire lives. Not me. I came from the backwoods of Virginia. I was country—all the way. Some of the guys used to make jokes about me coming from Gladys. They'd call me "Gladys Haley." And then I'd tell them, "No, you got it wrong. It was my cousin who was named Gladys. They named the town after her." I'd make up all kinds of crazy shit, just to play along. The truth was, I didn't know anything. I didn't know Roger Craig was one of the NFL's best running backs. I didn't know Ronnie Lott was one of the game's best defensive players. I'd never seen Jerry Rice score a touchdown. And I'd never seen Joe Montana throw a pass.

Veterans tend to prey on rookies like that—kids who seem out of place, unaware. Those poor suckers are subjected to the worst abuse, the nastiest hazing. I tried to compensate by acting tough and confident, just to protect myself, but it didn't always work. Once, during training camp, I was attacked by four or five guys in the locker room. Bubba Paris, a six-six, 305-pound offensive tackle, led the assault. At first I resisted, but these were some of the biggest, strongest players on the team. After a while I realized there was nothing I could do . . . so I gave up.

Those motherfuckers were crazy. They tied me to a bench with athletic tape—wrapped my whole body, like a mummy, so I couldn't move an inch. Then they took a jockstrap, stuck it in my mouth, and left my ass there. I couldn't believe it! Everyone was out on the field practicing, and I was being held hostage in the locker room, thinking I'd never get to play a down in a 49ers uniform.

Rookie hazing is like that, man. It's all meant in good fun, but it can be brutal. As humiliating as it was to be taped to a bench, it was nothing compared to what happened to me later that season. I was one of several players who had been asked to attend a luncheon in Pittsburg, a small town in Northern

California. This was an annual outing, and at the time they asked rookies to go along. I didn't realize at the time that some of the veterans—mainly Michael Carter and Dwaine Board—had arranged a nasty practical joke for me.

The night before the luncheon I'd had too much to drink. Eric Wright, one of my teammates, had let me borrow his car, and I had a little accident on the way home. I came around a curve, lost control for a moment, and went up on the curb. It was scary, but no one got hurt. I drove home real slow after that, happy to be alive.

We drove to Pittsburg the next day in a big van. On the way home, after the luncheon, I was sitting in the back, where rookies always sit. We were driving slowly through town when a local cop pulled us over. I had no idea what was going on. Everyone was acting real nervous, though. For days, the veterans had been talking about Pittsburg like it was Mississippi in the '60s; talking about how the cops were real rednecks who liked to throw black people in jail for no reason at all. Well, they had me going, man. I'm from the South, so it wasn't hard to get me to buy into that kind of behavior.

When the police officer asked everyone to get out of the van, I was prepared to be harassed. "I want to see some identification," he said.

We all started fumbling for our wallets. I handed him my driver's license. He stared at it for a moment, real hard. Then his eyes met mine.

"Mr. Haley, we have a warrant for your arrest on charges of hit-and-run driving."

I started shaking. *Holy shit! Did I hit somebody last night? Damn! Maybe I was drunker than I thought.* The cop put me up against the car, told me to spread my legs and put my hands behind my back. Then he slapped the cuffs on me and threw me in the patrol car. I sat there in total shock, not saying a word, whimpering a little bit, thinking maybe I had killed somebody. I was wondering what my mother was going to say.

Outside, the other guys were telling me they'd call one of the coaches, get me some help. Then they scrambled back into the van and followed us to the police station, which was only a few blocks away. Before we went in, the officer removed my cuffs, told me not to try anything stupid. In the station, though, the chief of police walked by, did a double-take when he saw me, and shouted, "Why isn't this man in handcuffs?!" Then he ran at me, grabbed me, and threw me up against a wall. I mean, he just *slammed* me!

And that's when everybody started laughing: the cops, the desk clerk, my teammates . . . all of them. People were laughing so hard they were falling down. It was all a setup, of course. Michael and Dwaine had arranged the whole thing with the cops, just to scare the shit out of me. Man, I was pissed.

"Go fuck yourselves!" I yelled. To me, it wasn't the slightest bit funny. Of course, if it had happened to somebody else, I probably would have been laughing, too. I just didn't like being the target of their jokes. But that's the price you pay when you're a rookie. It's all very confusing. You don't know who to trust, who to believe, who to respect.

You learn, though. You learn fast. You read the paper, you

watch the way people act during practice—the coaches and players—and pretty soon you understand the pecking order. In San Francisco, it wasn't hard to tell that Joe Montana was at the top.

Joe was different, though. He was a ball-buster, like most veterans, but in a good-natured sort of way. He treated everybody, including me, with total respect. I'd only been in training camp for about a week when he took me out to dinner. We stayed out till one in the morning, and he bought me drinks and we just sat there kicking and talking. I was impressed, man—impressed that he'd take the time to go out with a nobody like me, show me a good time. I never forgot that. From that day on, I was part of the Joe Montana fan club.

I just liked being around Joe. We used to autograph footballs together, after practice, and we'd stand there, looking like an odd couple—white quarterback, black linebacker—but we really had a lot in common. We both loved football, and we both liked to have fun. We'd bust each other all the time, make jokes about each other's personality and looks. I'd kill him about his nose, call him "Barry Manilow," or say, "Man, you sure your daddy wasn't Pinocchio?" Then Joe would fire right back at me, and when Joe started firing, everybody else jumped in. He was the leader—on the field and in the locker room.

It was like there were two Joe Montanas: the one the public saw, and the one I know. Joe wasn't the "quiet man" that he seemed to be. He was the life of the party. He was always up, always smiling, laughing, telling jokes—no matter how bad he was hurt, no matter how bad things were going on the field. He could always brighten up a day. But on the field he was all business. I'd see him get his ass beat—I mean just *whipped!* Hard enough to make a lesser man cry. And he'd just get up slowly and walk off the field. He'd never scream and yell at the offensive line. He'd never point a finger or embarrass anyone about screwing up. Instead, he'd walk calmly to the sideline and talk it over with Bill Walsh. You want to talk about control . . . Joe was *always* in control. I spent six years in San Francisco, and I never once saw the man panic. Joe was magic—pure magic.

The thing I remember most about the 1988 season, when I finally became a starter, was not any particular tackle or sack or anything else that I did. It was watching Joe work. That whole year Joe was just incredible. All he did was *dink and dunk*—screen passes, short slants, that kind of stuff—until the defense was so tight there was no room to breathe. Then, as soon as things loosened up—*bam!*—Joe would go for the home run.

That was the year of the Icky Shuffle Super Bowl in Miami. Icky Woods was a running back for the Cincinnati Bengals, and whenever he scored a touchdown he did this goofy little dance. The Bengals were 14–4 going into that game, and Icky was one of the most popular athletes in America. That dance allowed him to take his fifteen minutes of fame and stretch it out over six months. He was a good running back, though. And Boomer Esiason was a hell of a quarterback, a real tough son of a bitch, like Joe. Their defense was pretty good, too.

Still, going into the game we thought we had them beat. Joe had had a great season; Roger Craig was the NFC's Offensive Player of the Year; John Taylor and Jerry Rice were the receivers—what more do you need? I thought we'd run up the score on them.

But I was wrong. It turned out to be a great game, a real defensive battle. We kicked a field goal in the first quarter, they kicked one in the second. It was that kind of game. Jim Breach's last field goal, from forty yards out, gave the Bengals a 16–13 lead with 3:20 left in the game. I remember sitting on the sideline, watching the ball fly through the uprights, and thinking . . . *Fuck!* With Joe at quarterback, though, three minutes is a lot of time. Plenty of time. So I stood right up, took off my helmet, said a little prayer, and watched him go to work.

It was incredible. We started deep in our own territory, from the 8-yard line. But Joe was as cool as could be. *Dink and dunk . . . dink and dunk.* He kept pushing the ball down the field, eating up yardage with 5- and 10-yard bites. Finally, with about forty seconds left, we got to the 10-yard line. Joe threw a pass to John Taylor in the end zone, but one of their defenders came up under him and nearly picked it off. The ball hit the guy right in the hands, but he dropped it! For a second, I couldn't breathe. If he'd held onto the ball, the Bengals would have won the Super Bowl. Joe was smart, though. And fearless. He made the exact same call on the next play. And this time he hit JT in the back of the end zone for a touchdown. That was it . . . game over! We were world champions!

As far I'm concerned, that was not only the greatest Super

Bowl I've ever played in, but the greatest Super Bowl ever played, period. And the reason was Joe Montana.

Unfortunately, the 49ers underestimated Joe. They didn't think he'd be around as long as he was. I guess that's understandable—Joe had a lot of injuries, and by the time we won the Super Bowl after the '88 season, he was already thirty-two years old. But Joe was tough, as tough as any football player I've ever known. When the 49ers brought in Steve Young in 1987, Joe became more determined than ever to keep playing. Steve was an expensive insurance policy. He'd been a big star at Brigham Young in college; after that, instead of coming to the NFL, he signed a contract with the Los Angeles Express of the United States Football League for about a zillion dollars. When that league folded in 1985, he wound up in the NFL's version of hell: Tampa Bay. Two years later he was traded to San Francisco.

The idea, of course, was that Steve would be the backup until Joe retired. And if Joe got hurt, Steve would step in. I'm sure Steve thought Joe would be gone within a year or two. But Joe didn't make it easy for him—or for the 49ers. So they brought Steve in and paid him a lot of money to sit on the bench while Joe played. It seemed like every year there was talk about Joe retiring, and Steve taking over at quarterback. Then Joe would redo his contract and suit up for another season. And pretty soon Steve started to get pissed.

I understand what Steve was going through. He'd been the man wherever he was. He'd always been the star. And all of a sudden he was standing on the sidelines, charting plays.

Maybe he felt the frustration of being lied to . . . or misled . . . or whatever. But that's the way it goes. You just keep working, doing your job. You have to *earn* your playing time. You don't bad-mouth the guy in front of you—especially when that guy is one of the greatest quarterbacks ever to play the game. But that's what Steve did. He was always moping around the locker room, bad-mouthing Joe, stabbing him in the back. I never appreciated that at all, and neither did anyone else. The last couple years I was there the press tried to make it seem like there was a quarterback controversy: half the guys supporting Joe and half supporting Steve. But it wasn't like that at all. *Everybody* backed Joe. He had taken us there so many times. Even when his body tried to stop him from playing, Joe would go out there. He was a warrior, man, and everybody respected him for that. He had a good heart, too. He'd help anybody . . . even the guy who was trying to take his job.

Steve couldn't see any of that. He was such a whiner. The coaches would pacify him by letting him take half the snaps during practice—which, believe me, is un-fucking-heard of in the NFL; the starter usually gets 95 percent of the snaps—but even that wasn't enough for Steve. I used to look at him and think, *Man, you're already rich as shit from the USFL. Why don't you relax? The pressure is off. Your time will come.* I don't understand shit like that. Being a competitor is one thing, but being stupid is something else. And Steve Young is not a stupid man. The bottom line is, Joe Montana was an icon in San Francisco. He was a legend. And you don't treat a legend like that. You just don't do it.

Of course, Joe was a pro about the whole thing. He didn't talk about it much. Sometimes we'd be having a drink and he'd shake his head and say, "Man, it doesn't make sense." But that was about it. I'm just glad I wasn't there at the end, when Joe signed as a free agent with the Kansas City Chiefs. That must have been a sad day, because Joe did not belong in Kansas City. His career should have ended where it began: in San Francisco.

If Joe Montana was the heart of the 49ers during the 1980s, Ronnie Lott was the soul. Ronnie was not only the team's best defensive player; he was its conscience. His commitment to the team—to the *game*—was incredible. Ronnie was a mentor, an educator. He set a standard for everyone to follow. Ronnie is the reason I can go out and play in pain—because I watched him his whole career. He was awesome! He'd get knocked out, tear something, pull something, and he'd go right back in the game. At the most, he'd be out a few days and then come back, still hurting. Very few players have that kind of drive and dedication anymore. I was fortunate to be around him, to learn from a superstar.

I have to admit, though . . . I was a reluctant student at first. We played the Chargers in San Diego my rookie year, and they had an All-Pro tight end named Kellen Winslow. Kellen was a big, strong guy, and he knew all the tricks. He'd reach out and grab your jersey, pull you in tight so you couldn't move. The guy mugged the hell out of me the whole game. Our entire defense got beat up that day. I mean, the Chargers just *drove* us.

The next day was Monday, film day in the NFL. Everybody comes in, gets treatment, hangs out, and watches tape of the game. You don't really practice. You just let the wounds heal. Well, the whole defense was in one room together, watching the film, and Ronnie—that *motherfucker!*—stood up, pointed at the screen, and yelled . . . I mean, he just screamed: *"Charles! If I ever see you getting beat like that again, I'll kick your ass myself!"* And that was only the start of it. He really lit into me, tore me a new asshole right there in front of everyone. I was a rookie, so I sat there and swallowed it for a while. I bit my lip until it started to bleed. Finally, when I couldn't take it any longer, I got up and walked out of the room. I wanted to kill that little prick. I wanted to bust him up. In fact, for a while I tried to provoke him. I'd walk by his locker really slowly, hoping he'd bump into me or something. All I wanted was an excuse to rip his head off. I hated him.

Well, after about a week of this nonsense Ronnie walked over to me, got right up in my face, and said, "You want to whip my ass? Then go ahead . . . whip my ass. But if you want to be a better football player, then come with me."

I thought about it for a moment. It was a tough choice.

"Look," he said. "I know you're mad. But I'll tell you, man. I see something in you, and I want to help. You're too good to let somebody fool you the way that guy did."

I just sort of shrugged. But he had my attention now. Deep inside I knew Ronnie was a great football player. There was a level of respect I didn't really want to acknowledge, but it was definitely there. Ronnie worked hard—everybody could see that. He did all the drills, never sat one out. A lot of people like to talk the talk, but Ronnie . . . he walked the walk. So I thought, *Maybe I can learn something here. If not, I can always drill his sorry ass later.*

I decided to follow him out onto the field. And for the next hour he worked with me. He showed me how to take on blocks, and to fight them off. He made me realize that there's more to the game than brute strength or speed. You have to be smart. You have to know your opponent. Especially when you're playing the elephant position. Sometimes I'd be up like a linebacker, other times I'd be down like a lineman. Ronnie knew all the tricks. And he shared them with me.

I can honestly say that there are three reasons why I became a successful NFL player: 1) I was drafted by the 49ers; 2) Tommy Hart trained me and taught me how to be a pass rusher; 3) Ronnie Lott adjusted my attitude. After that incident, Ronnie and I clicked. Keena Turner used to say that Ronnie had a hellacious temper. Which he did. He could really fly off sometimes. But I didn't care. Shit, I was the same way. The more I got to know Ronnie, the more I realized what a special person he is. He's a very intelligent man. And he was always so serious about being the best football player he could possibly be. He was a teacher, but he was also a student. He never stopped learning. He'd start talking about guys I'd never even heard of. It was like he had a little book on everyone. He knew every player in the league and every college player coming out. He knew their strengths and weaknesses. Hell, I can't remember half the guys on my own team. I just walk by their lockers and go, "Hey, yo." People come and go like the wind in the NFL. If a guy's not a starter, I usually never get to know his name. But Ronnie was different. He had to know *everything*. He was into details.

Some people have accused Ronnie of being a dirty player. But he wasn't. He was just a *tough* player. Old school. We had a motto, me and Ronnie and a few other guys: *"Hit them and hit them hard."* When you knock them down, shake them a little bit. Let them see who you are, because you want it to stay in the back of their mind. If you hit them hard like that a few times, they'll start looking for a soft place to land when they see you coming. And then you *own* them! That's the way Ronnie played: with reckless abandon. When he hit you, he hit you with everything he had. When he blitzed, sometimes he'd come flying back out of that hole faster than he went in. But he didn't care. He was going to hit that hole again and again, no matter what. He believed in sacrificing everything.

The other thing about Ronnie—and you wouldn't know this from watching him on the football field—is that he's a really sensitive person. That fucker loves everybody: white, black, green, purple. Doesn't matter. Everybody brings their problems and lays them on Ronnie's shoulders, including me. You can call Ronnie up and he'll listen to your problems, and he won't interrupt. He'll just listen. When you're all finished—after you've poured your heart out—he'll say, "OK, now let's talk." But he won't tell you what to do. Instead, he'll say, "OK, what do *you* think you should do?" Most people just want to give you an opinion and get the hell off the phone. Ronnie finds a way to draw the right answer out of you.

He's strong; unfortunately, in San Francisco, his strength got him in trouble. Ronnie would go to bat for everybody. He got into confrontations with Bill Walsh, with George Seifert, with Eddie D., with Carmen. And by standing up for other people, he burned a few bridges. I saw other players use and manipulate Ronnie just because he had access to the coaches and the front office. I used to watch that shit and shake my head. I couldn't understand why he'd risk his career for people who didn't really give a damn about him. Ronnie had a big heart. Maybe too big.

The other player I really admired when I was in San Francisco was Jerry Rice. Jerry was the NFC Player of the Year in 1987 and MVP of Super Bowl XXIII, when we beat the Bengals. In my opinion he's the greatest wide receiver ever to play the game. He's sleek and fast and just about unstoppable. And he works as hard as anyone I've ever known; his off-season training sessions are legendary. Guys would visit Jerry and try to work out with him and they'd be puking their guts up after twenty minutes. He's always in phenomenal shape.

I like Jerry a lot. He's good people. Sometimes I pick on him, though, because he's almost too perfect. He does everything beautifully, elegantly. When he runs, he looks great. When he gets hit, he looks great. When he's pulling himself up on all fours after getting his lights turned out, he looks great. He can be half unconscious, staggering around, and he'll take the time to straighten his uniform, brush the dirt off his jersey. Whenever we play the 49ers I always tell everyone, "Mess up Jerry's clothes—that'll fuck him up." I figure by the time he puts his uniform back in order, maybe the play will be over. That's as good a way as any to stop him.

You see, Jerry's a very meticulous person. He's dressed so sharp all the time—head to toe. Most wide receivers are like that. They always dress up. I've never yet met a high-profile wide receiver who dressed like a bum. Even in casual clothes these guys look fantastic. They make sweats look like high fuckin' fashion.

I used to get a kick out of Jerry's locker. Mine would be a mess: shit strewn all over the place, funky smell. But Jerry's was so neat, man—everything in order. And he always had a little flunky around, blowing his nuts, telling him how great he was. It wasn't necessarily a young player, either. Sometimes it was a new guy who wanted to kick it with Jerry Rice; someone who wanted to hang out with a star. They knew their job. They knew what was expected. Jerry was the man, and they were supposed to help make him feel like the man.

When I left, Jamie Williams was the flunky. I don't know who it is now. But I feel for the guy, whoever it is. Kissing someone's ass all season is hard work—even when that ass is as clean as Jerry Rice's.

Charles in Charge, Part III
MAD ABOUT MADDEN

I first met John Madden in 1987, during my second season with the 49ers. We hit it off right away, and we've been friends ever since. I have enormous respect for John. He was one of the smartest and most successful coaches in the NFL, a man who really knew the game and how to treat his players. I would love to have played for him. He was the kind of coach who expected his players to do their job, and to do it well. From what I understand—and I've talked to several people who played for him—he was an extremely demanding, but fair, coach. As long as you performed at a high level, he stayed off your back. That's my kind of coach.

Today, of course, most people know John from his television work. He's the best color commentator in the business. Puts everyone else to shame. The broadcast booths these days are filled with ex-coaches and ex-players, people who know a lot about football, but don't have any idea how to communicate with the average viewer; guys who think they're so smart that they don't even bother to do their homework. John knows how to entertain and inform. I think the reason he's so popular is that he sounds just like you would if you were sitting at home trying to do the commentary yourself. He gets all excited, yells *"wham!"* and *"oooh!"* on big hits, just like the typical fan. It's like he could be right there in your living room, sitting next to you. He makes the game come alive.

John has achieved his success without selling his soul. He won't badmouth a player just because he makes a ton of money. You hear a lot of that from broadcasters now. It's common to find someone in the booth who's bitter because he played or coached at a time when salaries weren't as high as they are now. Well, too bad. That shouldn't cloud your judgment. John never lets that kind of thing get in the way. He calls it just like it is. If a guy's not playing hard, or if he's not playing as well as he used to play, John will tell the viewer. Straight-out. But he won't sit there and belittle players just because he doesn't like them. Most commentators take shots at players just for the hell of it. They're only concerned about their own careers. John cares about the game. He cares about being honest.

What I'm trying to say is that John Madden is a real person. He reports the truth without dwelling on the negative. You won't hear him harping about player suspensions or off-field incidents. He tries to concentrate on the football part of it—because that's his job. When a professional athlete gets in trouble, everybody in the world knows about it. It doesn't take any particular talent or expertise to point that shit out. When a television commentator starts babbling about a player's personal problems, that tells me one thing: He doesn't have anything else to talk about. He's either unprepared, mean-spirited, or just plain stupid.

Most of the players I know feel the same way. They all love John Madden. Each year he picks his own personal all-star team, the All-Madden Team, and most players consider inclusion to be one of the biggest honors in football. John is from the old school. He likes players who get the job done by any means necessary, and those are the players he picks to his team. They're all talented, but they're also tough as hell. They're *football* players—in the truest sense of the word. They don't mind getting dirty or bloodied. They play hard on every snap of the ball. And they play hurt. They're *iron men*.

I've made the All-Madden team four times, and I take more pride in that than in any of the other awards I've won. Making the Pro Bowl, All-Pro, stuff like that—it's all very political. Voting is done by the media, and factors that have nothing to do with football are taken into consideration. A lot of guys won't play that game. They want to be judged by what they do on the field, not whether they give great interviews or whatever else. That's why they cherish the All-Madden award. Each year John gives something different to the players on his team. Sometimes it's a trophy. Sometimes it's a jersey or a jacket or a sweatsuit. And I'll tell you . . . guys wear that stuff with pride. It means something.

The bottom line with John—the reason I like him so much—is that he's a decent human being, as well as a great coach and broadcaster. We talk for hours sometimes. I feel like I can tell him anything. He's one of the few people whose advice I sought when I started thinking about retirement. He told me, "Charles, play as long as you can, because when it's over, it's over. There's nothing quite like being a football player. So make sure you have no regrets when you call it quits."

He also told me if I ever needed a job, I could always be his driver. See, John doesn't like to fly. He travels all over the country in a big, customized bus known as the *Madden Cruiser*.

You never know—I may take him up on the offer someday.

Chapter 6

Jimmy and Jerry

When I arrived at the airport in Dallas, Rich Dalrymple, the Cowboys' director of media relations, was there to greet me. And so was Jerry Jones. That was a shock. I didn't expect the team's owner to take such a hands-on approach. I was impressed. I guess he wanted to meet the guy who was earning more than Troy Aikman and Emmitt Smith. You see, when I came to Dallas in late August, 1992, I was the highest-paid player on the team. But I wasn't worried about the money. To me, it's always been about the game. That's what matters. I want to be paid, of course, and I want to be paid well. More than anything else, though, I want to win.

I sensed right away that Jerry felt the same way. He seemed to be a straight shooter. We took a long ride back to the hotel, and he kept reassuring me the whole way that this trade would work out for the best.

"You're the missing piece, Charles," he said. "I've heard all the stories, all the accusations, and I'm not concerned. You're gonna be one of my guys."

I found it easy to talk to Jerry. I told him that I understood I was coming in under awkward circumstances. "All I want is a chance," I said. "Treat me like a man, respect me as an athlete. That's all I ask. Just treat me fairly."

Jerry smiled. "No problem."

That ride from the airport did a lot to boost my spirits. At the time I was in a bit of a funk. I knew I had to leave San Francisco—I could see it coming months ahead of time. It was like when I left high school and went to college. I had to get out. And, just like when I left Gladys, people kept telling me I'd fail. They said if I went to another team, I'd probably get cut or something. I was determined not to let that happen.

It was one of the strangest times of my life. I was at the top of my game. I was twenty-eight years old. I had two Super Bowl rings. I'd played in three Pro Bowls. I was supposed to have the world by the balls. But all of a sudden everyone was doggin' me, saying, *"He's more trouble than he's worth."* I was baffled by the criticism, because I felt like my only fault was that I cared too much. I gave 110 percent every time I went out on the field. I never slacked off. *Never!*

Apparently, though, that wasn't enough for the 49ers, and now my life was a mess. I had to start all over with a new team. On top of that, I was worried about my marriage falling apart because my wife loved California and did not want to move to Dallas. When Bill McPherson asked me to apologize to Seifert, Karen was backing him up, telling me to go with the flow. She's a military woman, and she doesn't believe in bucking the system. "Sorry," I said. "I have to go." Karen stayed behind for a while, along with our daughter, Princess, and our son, Charles Jr. That was tough. I missed them a lot. But it gave us time to think. And it gave me time to concentrate on becoming a Cowboy.

A Cowboy.

I didn't really know what that meant at the time. Soon enough, though, I'd find out.

I quickly discovered that when it came to professional sports, Dallas was nothing like San Francisco. Fans in the Bay Area are very cool, laid-back. In Dallas, they're fucking crazy. I don't mean that as an insult. The Cowboys have the greatest fans in the world, but they are obsessed. The entire state of Texas lives and breathes the Cowboys. You could walk into the lion's den at the zoo and the lion would say, "Uh, can I have your autograph?" For me, it was quite an adjustment. Whenever I went out people seemed to recognize me. I was making a lot of money and I was a big-time football player— but I'd never really felt like a *star*. Until now. Fortunately, the fans in Dallas made me feel welcome. They'd call in to talk radio shows and say, "Give Haley a break, will ya?" The media, of course, went after me right from the start. I had a bad reputation because of some of the things that had occurred in San Francisco, and I fanned the fire by refusing to cooperate with reporters in Dallas. But I didn't care about the media. Never have, never will. As long as I had the respect of my teammates and the support of the fans, I thought everything would work out just fine.

I met with head coach Jimmy Johnson on my second day in Dallas, first thing in the morning. I tried to go in with an open mind, because I'd gotten all kinds of conflicting reports about him—as a person and a coach. What I'd heard, mainly, was that he was an asshole and a racist. I had heard stuff like that from players who called me up right before I left San Francisco. "Watch your back," they said. "He'll go after you." But one of my teammates on the 49ers, Kevin Fagan, a defensive end who had played for Jimmy at the University of Miami, said something else: "If you're one of Jimmy's guys, he'll take care of you." It turned out that Kevin was more correct than anyone else.

My introduction to Jimmy was uneventful. It was a very basic, rah-rah kind of meeting. He told me what he expected, I told him how I wanted to be treated. We shook hands; he said, "Welcome aboard," and I went on my way. No big deal. Not long after that, though, I got to see Jimmy in action. We had a team meeting, and he stood up there and started talking . . . just talking a mile a minute, the way he does when he gets excited. This was the preseason, when guys were still fighting for jobs and playing time, so Jimmy had everyone's attention.

"You are not all equal," he said. "Not in my eyes. Some of you I will treat as though you belong up here," and he lifted his hand head-high. "And the rest of you motherfuckers . . .

I'll treat down here." He lowered his hand slowly, until it was even with his crotch. As I watched this little show, the first thought that entered my mind was . . . *This is going to be interesting.*

It didn't take long to get excited about my new job prospects. Gary Clark had told me that the Cowboys had enough talent to win the Super Bowl. As a wideout for the Redskins, he'd gotten to know the Cowboys up close and personal over the last few seasons. "They have more raw talent than you can believe," Gary had said. "You're gonna get another ring, man." A lot of other people thought so, too. The Cowboys had been rebuilding since '89, when Jerry bought the team and hired Jimmy as the head coach. They were quite a pair. Co-captains of the football team at the University of Arkansas back in the '60s, they'd since gone their separate ways: Jerry into the oil business, Jimmy into coaching—first at Oklahoma State, then at Miami. Each was a proven winner: Jerry had a whole shitload of money; Jimmy had a whole shitload of victories. And now the two old Razorbacks were reunited. They had promised to revive the franchise, and they were starting to make good on that promise. Good thing, too, because an awful lot of Cowboys fans had never forgiven Jerry for firing Tom Landry. Landry was the Cowboys' first coach. Until Jimmy came in, he was the *only* coach. He was God's coach, as someone once said. So there was a lot of pressure on these guys.

It took a few years—the Cowboys won only one game in 1989 and seven in 1990—but after making the playoffs with an 11–5 record in 1991, Jimmy and Jerry had turned the corner. A lot of their top draft picks—guys like Troy and Emmitt and Michael Irvin—were starting to look like superstars. Everything was coming together; I could see that after just a few days of practice. This team was loaded! And I was part of it. For the first time in quite a while, I felt lucky.

Right from the start, I liked the way Jerry Jones ran his business. In fact, I still do. A lot of people think Jerry is all about the money, especially after he negotiated his own deal with Nike; boy, did that piss off the NFL brass. They think he's this wild maverick who only cares about lining his own pockets and defying the system. But that's not true. Jerry wants to make the system *better*. You have to remember—he invested just about everything he had to buy the Dallas Cowboys. So this isn't a hobby for him; it's his livelihood.

One of the things I really like about Jerry is that he has a heart. He's made mistakes and he's learned from them. He's human. He knows his players are human, too. Jerry is the kind of guy who comes to practice every day, because he likes to know what's going on with his team—he told the world a long time ago that he wasn't going to give away his money blindly. But when he's there, he's always in a good mood. He's always joking, talking . . . *communicating*. He's accessible, more so than any other owner I've ever known. And he has a sense of humor. If a player walks by and Jerry starts talking to him, everybody will start making disgusting noises—*Slurp! Slurp!*— like he's giving Jerry a blowjob or something. But it's all in good fun. We do stuff like that all the time. Jerry just laughs and wiggles his finger and says, "Uh-uh," like we're a bunch of little kids.

———

I watched the last preseason game and then started working out with the team. One week later we beat the Redskins 23–10 in a nationally televised Monday night game. I didn't start, but I played quite a bit; even got a sack and forced a fumble, which was kind of nice. The plan was to watch me move for a few weeks, see how I adjusted to my new position, defensive end, and how quickly I picked up a new system. But the Cowboys' system was so easy to learn, I could have done it from day one. They only had three or four different defenses. If you played the D-line, all you had to know was the first part, and then you were done. I tried to learn other positions just so I could stay awake in team meetings. I guess I should thank George Seifert for that. There were so many different defenses in San Francisco, so many different combinations and blitzes, I had to really study to stay on top of my game. By the time I got to Dallas, it was easy.

The second week we beat the Giants 34–28. I started that game. After just two weeks, the job was mine. I was comfortable, and we were on a roll. Already, though, I was at the center of a controversy. Before I even played a game for the Cowboys, an ESPN reporter, Fred Edelstein, went on the air and reported that I had tried to provoke Troy Aikman. Supposedly, I had cornered Troy in the locker room and made some comment about him not being half the quarterback Joe

Montana was. Complete fucking bullshit! Never happened. I was new to the team. I was trying to keep a low profile. The last thing I wanted to do was come in and piss off the quarterback before I'd even played a game. But that's the way the media works—they say what they want to say, whether it's true or not.

The truth is, Troy was a promising young quarterback then. But he had a lot to learn. He still has a lot to learn. I don't think you can compare him to Joe Montana. Not yet. But then, almost no one can withstand that comparison. Troy has become a very good quarterback. He's a fierce competitor. And he's a winner—I think he's proven that. I just wish he'd loosen up a little bit. Troy is so damn serious. Hardly ever smiles. He's a good-looking guy with a ton of money. He ought to be having more fun.

We won our first three games in '92 before getting our butts kicked by the Eagles in the fourth week. That was a reality check, and it helped us get back to work. We pretty much steamrolled the rest of the year. We went 13–3 in the regular season and hammered everyone in the playoffs. It was especially sweet for me because we beat the 49ers in the NFC title game. That was payback time.

In the Super Bowl we kicked the shit out of the Buffalo Bills, 52–17. I had six tackles—and one very big sack. The Bills actually scored first, took a 7–0 lead ten minutes into the game. Then Troy threw a touchdown pass to Jay Novacek to make it 7–7. With about a minute and a half left in the first quarter, I hit Jim Kelly, the Bills' quarterback, from the blind side just as he was about to pass. They were deep in their own territory, at the two-yard line, and the ball popped loose. Jimmie Jones picked it out of the air and ran in for the touchdown. That started the mudslide right there. It was the turning point of the game. Two hours later I had my third Super Bowl ring.

Not that I ever wear them. I try not to wallow in the past, so I rarely put my rings on. My wife keeps them hidden in a safe deposit box somewhere. I don't even want them in my house. The less I think about them, the more I win. I guess that's superstitious, but it's the way I feel. Most guys like to wear their rings, especially when they're out at night, in another city. Super Bowl rings are big suckers, and they do attract the ladies. But that's not for me. I'd rather look ahead than behind.

Jimmy and I got along pretty well my first year; with the exception of one or two little incidents, it was kind of like a honeymoon period. He was definitely a get-in-your-face kind of coach, as I expected. But that didn't concern me. As long as he didn't try to get in *my* face, we were fine. I just did my job. I was always motivated. The guys who weren't motivated had trouble with Jimmy, because he was pretty fucking intense every day—in meetings, in practice, in games. He'd start drills over in a heartbeat if guys weren't working hard. He'd just say, "Do it again! Now!" And then we'd try again. It was like a really tough, physical training camp all season long with Jimmy. And he got the results he wanted.

The thing you have to admire about Jimmy—regardless of how you feel about him personally—is that he has a big set of balls. He'll take chances. Most coaches aren't willing to do that. They're scared to death of fucking up, of making a mistake that will cost them their job. Jimmy always kept the other team off balance. Sometimes he'd take a chance, run a crazy play just for the hell of it, because he believed in his team and he believed in his players. And, of course, he believed in himself. And when the guys saw that, they started believing, too. It's such a simple thing, but most coaches never pick up on it. Jimmy did. He'd make those crazy-ass calls: fake field goals, fake punts. *Fourth-and-two? Let's go for it!*

No doubt about it, man, Jimmy was inspiring. He also acted somewhat insane from time to time, and sometimes his motivational tactics backfired. Like if a player jumped offside, he'd get right in the guy's face and start screaming, "You ever do that again and you'll never play another fuckin' down for the Dallas Cowboys!" That works with some people, but it's a big mistake with others. You end up with a guy sitting back on his heels, terrified of screwing up, playing at half speed.

Jimmy's halftime tirades could be brutal. He'd undress people, man—insult them so badly that we'd have to spend the third quarter boosting them back up. And if you played like a pussy on Sunday, you could be damn sure Jimmy was going to point it out to the whole team on Monday, when we were watching film. He loved to humiliate people.

I have to admit there were times I enjoyed watching Jimmy's act. Kenny Norton, who was a starting linebacker for the Cowboys at the time, and a real prima donna, walked away from a tongue-lashing during a game once, and the next day at practice Jimmy met him at the door and got right up under that long chin of his. Jimmy was just screaming—his face was flushed, his eyes were all bloodshot; I think his hair even moved. And Kenny had to stand there and take it. I loved that one. There's no doubt that Jimmy gets borderline players to perform at a different level. The thing is, you have to do it right. You have to strike a balance. I don't think Jimmy was able to do that, especially my second year there, 1993.

I like the fact that he insisted that guys work. He stayed on top of the coaches as well as the players. But he never showed people that he cared about them as human beings. That was the one thing I didn't like.

"I'm extremely pleased with the practice and attitude of Charles Haley. He's taken on the leadership role with the young guys, guys like (defensive linemen) Leon Lett, Tony Hill, Russell Maryland, Jimmie Jones, and Chad Hennings.

"For a guy who has had as much success as Charles Haley, that says something. I don't think it's any surprise that we became number one in the league in defense after we traded for Charles. That's not to take anything away from the other defensive players because we have some fine ones. I just think Charles played a big role in us becoming the top defense."

—JIMMY JOHNSON, AUGUST 1993

Maybe Jimmy was blowing smoke when he made that statement to a bunch of newspaper reporters the summer after we won the Super Bowl. Or maybe he was misquoted. God knows that happens often enough. More likely, though, it was just a matter of the honeymoon not being quite over yet. Because in the next few months, he and I went at it. Jimmy started to get on my nerves, and I'm sure I got on his.

Everyone expected us to win a second straight Super Bowl. We were two or three deep at every position. Our confidence was soaring. If you looked at it realistically, there was no reason for us *not* to repeat. So it was quite a shock when we lost our first two games. First, the Redskins hammered us, 35–16. Then the Bills got a little revenge for the Super Bowl with a 13–10 victory. There we were, the defending Super Bowl champions, with an 0–2 record. Jimmy got everyone going, though. That whole season, whenever the team was down, Jimmy would stand up in front of the media and *guarantee* a win. And his strategy, fucked up as it was, seemed to work. We got on a roll, won the next seven games to take over first place in the NFC East. We lost two more games in November, to Atlanta and Miami, but finished up with five straight victories. By the end of the regular season we were 12–4 and on a definite high heading into the playoffs.

For me, though, it was a difficult year. My back had been bothering me since late June, and I played with a fair amount of pain all season. It was tolerable most of the time. I could control it, but I knew it was serious. When I went to see Dr.

Robert Watkins, a Los Angeles back specialist, he said I had herniated a disk, and suggested that surgery would take care of the problem. But I wanted to wait until after the season.

In addition to my physical problems, I was knocking heads with Jimmy. We had a real nasty run-in up in Minnesota. We won the game, but when I got into the locker room afterward, Jimmy was bitching out the team. As I walked in he looked right at me and yelled, "Get your ass in here!" So I just kept on walking. I figured I'd ignore him, let him blow off a little steam. But then he screamed again.

"Stand still when I'm talking to you!"

Well, that was too much. I was stunned that he'd talk to me like that, like I was a punk. I was so pissed that I walked all the way up to the podium, really slowly, and stood right in front of his face. I stared at him until he was finished. Jimmy wasn't intimidated, though. He kept ranting and raving, cursing everyone out. When he was through he went into his dressing room. I went right in after him, and we had us a little talk. Jimmy said I was one of the guys he respected most, but that he needed me to be able to stand there and take a tongue-lashing once in a while. I told him that was bullshit; respect goes two ways. You don't just jump on someone's ass when they don't know what the hell is going on.

After a while we ran out of things to say. I walked out and went back over to my locker. About ten minutes later Jerry Jones walked by with a smile on his face. He leaned into me and said, real quietly, "Don't worry, Charles. He ain't gonna cut you."

I wasn't worried about that. I'd signed a new contract before the start of the season, and I was one of the highest paid defensive linemen in the league. No way they were going to cut me; trade me, perhaps, but not cut me. That incident did, however, make me realize that Jerry and Jimmy were definitely not on the same page. Everyone kind of suspected from the beginning that things were going on behind the scenes; that Jimmy and Jerry didn't always get along so well. They had a way in public, and around us, of making everything seem like it was okay. You know, they'd smile, pat each other on the back, act like best buddies.

But it was all just a big show.

———

I missed two games completely in '93 and had to come off the bench in three others. My back was deteriorating as the season went on. My playing time was limited, and I could hardly practice at all. By the playoffs, though, I was back in the starting lineup. We played the 49ers in the NFC championship game again, and there was no way I was going to miss that one. Whenever we played the 49ers I took it personally. I felt that they had done me wrong, so I tried to vent my frustration and anger. Those games were hard for me. After ten plays I'd be dead tired because I was playing on pure emotion—anger, hate—instead of concentrating on doing the things I was supposed to do. But I usually calmed down after a while.

It was important for me to have a good playoff game against the 49ers, and I did. I knocked down one pass and picked up a sack. The 49ers did everything they could to slow down our pass rush—they even used a running back for pass blocking purposes on just about every play—but we really beat up on Steve Young that day. Our whole defense was flying. So was the offense. We won easily, 38–21, and then beat the Bills—again—in Super Bowl XXVIII. It was a little closer this time, 30–13, but still not much of a game.

In two years with the Cowboys I'd won two Super Bowls. I had four rings altogether. There wasn't much room for celebration, though. In the weeks leading up to the Super Bowl I knew that it was only a matter of time before I'd have to deal with my chronically sore back. I couldn't ignore it any longer.

I had back surgery for the first time on February 8, 1994. Dr. Watkins performed a microscopic lumbar diskectomy, which means he removed a small piece of one of the disks in my back. The disk had ruptured and was putting pressure on the nerves around my spinal cord. The pain was excruciating. I'd had knee injuries, groin injuries, shoulder injuries—all the usual football shit—but I'm telling you, there's nothing like back pain, nerve pain. There's no way to cut it. You just deal with it.

At the time, though, I was still reasonably young and healthy. I had just turned thirty years old, and Dr. Watkins was confident that the surgery was a success. With a little luck, I'd be back on the field in a few months, playing at full strength.

Playing for a new coach, too. The power struggle between

Jimmy and Jerry went on right through the Super Bowl and escalated in the weeks afterward. On March 29, 1994, Jimmy announced his resignation. That way he was allowed to save face. The truth, though, was that somebody forgot who owned the damn team. Somebody thought he was bigger than the team. Jimmy always used to tell us, "The team is bigger than any single player." That was one of his favorite sayings. I guess he forgot that the team is also bigger than the coach; and the owner is bigger than the team.

I think what happened to Jimmy is that he got caught up in all the hype. He started believing his own press. Everyone told him how great he was, and he started thinking he could do anything he wanted and get away with it. He wanted complete control of the team—personnel decisions, draft choices, everything. There was no way Jerry was going to give him that. They were playing poker, and in the end I think Jerry used his ace in the hole: He *fired* Jimmy's ass.

Charles in Charge, Part IV
MUSIC AND MAYHEM

Everyone has a game-day routine, a way to deal with the fear and anxiety that comes with being a professional football player. Some guys meditate. Some guys use speed. Some guys butt heads. Some guys puke.

Me? I like cartoons.

We always stay in a hotel the night before a game—even the home games. They say sex can take your legs away, so we get locked up in a hotel room, away from our wives or girlfriends. Seems pretty stupid to me, especially since a lot of guys sneak women in anyway. It's a tradition, though, and it makes the coaches feel like they're doing all they can to keep players out of trouble.

Some guys don't sleep well the night before a game. I sleep like a baby. And when I wake up, I reach for the remote and find my cartoons. I love cartoons, man. Just fuckin' love 'em. Every time a cartoon video comes out, I buy it, and then my wife says, "You're not buying that for the kids; you're buying it for yourself." Which is not entirely true. I love watching cartoons *with* my kids. When I was real little, we didn't even have a TV. So maybe I'm making up for lost time. It's the kid in me trying to come out. Cartoons remind you that it's okay to be young and to laugh. It's okay to just be a kid.

A lot of players on the 49ers used to kid me about it, but I didn't care. There aren't a lot of things I'll fight for, but I'll fight for my right to watch cartoons, no matter how old I am. My favorite is Bugs Bunny, because he's a smart-ass. Bugs is always trying to get away with shit . . . just like me.

We usually take a bus to the stadium a few hours before game time. I listen to music on the way, mostly rhythm and blues, old Motown stuff. (I can tell I'm getting old, because I don't understand a lot of rap, although I kind of like Tupac and Dr. Dre.) I also like to know who's scared and who's not scared. If I look in a guy's eyes, and I can see that he's scared, I'll try to build him up. I'll walk him through a dream, talk about his opponent's strengths and weaknesses. I'll say, "The bottom line is attitude. Do not blink at him. If he wants to look at you, look him dead in the eye and do not say a word. Let him know you mean business. And when the game begins, one of two things will happen: Either you'll whip his ass or he'll whip yours. If you want to be a punk—if you want to be embarrassed in front of your wife and your kids and your mom and dad, that's on you. But if you want to do this right, we'll do it together."

By the time we get to the stadium, they've got their confidence. They're ready to play. It's amazing. I take great pride in that.

In the locker room I'm usually talkin', talkin', talkin'. I've got all this nervous energy, and I can't stop. They used to tell me, "Charles, will you please shut the fuck up?! You're making it hard for other players to get prepared." And I'd be like, "Shit, man, this is the way *I* prepare. Can't I get a little consideration?" The 49ers locker room was like a morgue, everyone was so serious. That ain't the way I play football. I sit in there and crack jokes. I try to keep everyone loose. If I'm really on, I can get Troy laughing so hard that he chokes on his damn tobacco. He's always sitting there with a big cloud over his head, all gloomy and shit, until I get him going. Troy sits right in front of the training room, so he's the first person you see when you come through the door, and I just can't resist fucking with him.

About an hour before the game, all the humor drains out of me. It just gets sucked away. That's when I get my armor together. My armor protects me, so I'm careful with it. I make sure everything is in place. I put my tape on my shoulder pads. I pull my jersey down. Most players get the equipment managers to handle that stuff, but I like to do it myself. It's personal. When I touch the armor I can feel the anguish, the pain. I know I'm getting ready for battle. When I rub those pads, man, it calms me down. It makes me loose.

Players do different things in that last hour; strange things. Deion Sanders likes to lay out his whole uniform: jersey on top, pants, socks, gloves where his hands are supposed to be. Up at the head he'll have one of those little scarves instead of a helmet. He walks around the locker room telling people not to mess with it, because it'll bring him bad luck. A couple times I've kicked his shit all over the place, just to watch him freak.

I have a small group of guys I like to huddle with before each game: Tony Tolbert, Leon Lett, Godfrey Myles. We call ourselves "Mandinka Warriors," and each week we put our hands together and repeat one word over and over. It's a different word every game. We choose it early in the week, to help prepare for the battle, the bloodshed. We think about it each day in practice:

Violence . . . Mission . . . Destruction . . .

Sounds awful, huh? But that's the attitude you need on the football field. It's not a game for the weak. You have to have one personality on the field and another personality off the field. Only a fool goes out there happy and smiling. He's the guy they take off on a stretcher. If you stay focused, if you stay in a violent mood, you're less likely to get hurt.

Maim . . . Mutilate . . . Death . . .

These are ugly words, but we use them to define the sport, to remind ourselves that it's a very serious game. I remember a representative from the NFL offices came in once and gave a speech of some kind. At one point he said, "Football is not a violent sport." I don't know what he said next, because I left the meeting at that point.

It's weird. In that moment before you leave the locker room, it's like you're preparing for an execution. And you don't know whether you're the hangman or a dead man walkin'. But when you run through that tunnel, and half your teammates are already out there on the field, and you hear the crowd—that unbelievable fucking *ROAR!* of 66,000 people in Texas Stadium —there is nothing in the world like it. You're flying through the tunnel, like Superman, and then you're on the field, giving people five, bumping chests, soaking up the noise. It's an incredible experience. To me, that's the best part of the game. Just that little moment. I love it.

CHAPTER 7

Love and Marriage

Family is the most important thing in the world to me—and my family starts with my mom. I love my wife to death, but there's a woman back in Gladys named Virginia Haley, and she's my biggest hero. She brought me into this world and she stood behind me through good times and bad. She took care of me for the first twenty years of my life, so I've got a whole bunch of love for her.

A lot of players in the NFL are "momma's boys." Maybe it's because so many pro athletes come from poor backgrounds, from single-parent homes. I don't know. I can only tell you that there's a very deep sense of loyalty and love. Unfortunately, some NFL wives are jealous of the relationship their husbands have with their mothers. I know a lot of guys who talk about it. They'll come into the locker room, pissing and moaning about how they want to do something special for their mom, but they have to do it on the sly, because they don't want to start a fight at home. I go through it too, and I think it's ridiculous. I mean, this is my mom! I love her and I want to take care of her. It's not a contest. Some wives think you're trying to buy love or whatever, but it's not like that at all. It's an *obligation*. You're supposed to help your parents if you can. They did everything for you when you were a child, and if you're in a position to pay them back, you should. I've been lucky. I've made some money. So I'm going to take care of my family, especially my mom. I call her all the time. I go back to visit. My mom loves to go get all dressed up and go to church, so I buy her shoes and dresses and coats. It makes her happy.

Sometimes my wife understands my attachment to my mother. Sometimes she doesn't. She'll get angry or start teasing me. She'll quote the Bible: "You know, it says a man is supposed to leave home to cling to a woman, and then she becomes his new family." But you can find anything you want in the Bible if you look hard enough. It also says in the Bible that you're supposed to love your mother. And I do.

They say it's not unusual for a man to marry his mother. Not literally, of course. But he chooses a woman who reminds him of his mother. I think I did that. In a lot of ways, Karen is just like my mom. She's tough, which is probably why we're still married. She's a smart, no-nonsense woman who doesn't take shit from anyone, including me. Karen will speak her mind. If you cross her, she'll get right up in your face, and she won't back down. I think her attitude comes from being in the military for so long—four years of ROTC in college, three years after that. Karen was a captain, and captains like to give orders; she likes to tell people what to do; she's combative.

You don't shake that military influence right away, believe me. I live with it every day. Our lives are completely regimented. Up at a certain time, in bed at a certain time, eat at a certain time. If I take the kids out to play or to a movie or something, and they end up getting off schedule, it's like I committed murder or something. Karen gets all flustered, starts yelling, "No! No! It's gotta be like this!" I get lectured all the time about being more organized, responsible. Karen will take my life apart and put it back together in a heartbeat. She thinks she knows exactly what I need and don't need; what I should say and what I shouldn't say. Sometimes I'll just tune her right out. I won't even hear what she's saying, but I know she's saying a lot.

Funny thing is, my mom was the same way. She used to do a lot of screaming and hollering when we were kids. My mom never backed down from my dad, and now my wife doesn't back down from me. Of course, my mom is a lot bigger than my wife. Karen is only five-two. But the way she talks . . . *shit!* You'd think she was seven-two. She's fearless.

My wife is feisty, which has been both a blessing and a

curse in our marriage. Sometimes I wish I could get Karen to put on a skirt once in a while and let me wear the pants in the family. But at least I know she's strong; if something were to happen to me, I wouldn't have to worry about her or my children. They'd be just fine. As it is, she's a big help financially. She would never make an investment without my approval, but she does more background work on it than I do. If we're thinking about investing some money, she'll read a ton of background material, research it to death. Not me. I can retain knowledge when someone gives a presentation or something, but I'm not interested in doing a lot of homework. I'm careful with my money. I'm conservative. Most of my investment decisions are based on simply being cautious. But Karen takes it a step further. She analyzes and studies and plans. She enjoys that kind of work. She likes to keep everything in perfect order. That's why the filing cabinets in our home are all organized. Karen keeps everything: bills, mail, magazines from a hundred years ago. I'll be throwing stuff away as fast as I can and she'll be digging it out of the trash can.

The truth is this: My wife and I do not have a perfect marriage. But I don't know anyone who does. We have our disagreements, just like most couples. We always manage to work through our problems, though. Even when I get mad at my wife, I know how lucky I am to be married to her. If it weren't for Karen, I'd probably be in prison. At best I'd be bouncing from team to team, with no kind of career. It's my tendency to be a little wild, but Karen keeps me in line. If I'm out running with the boys in the streets or something, she'll confront me. And if I don't listen to what she's trying to tell me, she'll just say, "Hey, I'm out of here!" Let me tell you, that's enough to make you take a deep breath and back up a step or two.

Losing my wife would hurt me terribly. I've been married for ten years, and I still love her. I can't even imagine trying to find another woman, someone who will understand me. That would take a lifetime, because I'm not the easiest person to live with. And anyway, it's almost impossible for a professional athlete to find someone he can trust. You can't just believe somebody loves you for who you are, unless you accidentally stumble into Montana or someplace like that, where nobody knows who you are and they don't give a shit about the NFL. Either that or you have to find someone who has just as much money as you do, which isn't likely. That wasn't the case with me and Karen. Money had nothing to do with our relationship. We were kids when we met. *Poor* kids.

After all this time, Karen pretty much understands me. She understands my moods and she does her best to tolerate them. She gives me room when I come in the house. She lets me unwind before we start a conversation. She knows when I come home from practice or a game that I like to be by myself for a little while. I like to play with the computer, just chill out. Then I play with the kids. And after the kids go to bed, Karen and I talk about the day. If there's something we need to discuss, we get it out in the open.

Everybody grows up different. I'm a family type of person. Always have been. I need family around me. Football players are supposed to be tough, fearless, but the one thing that really frightens me is being alone. I'm scared of divorce because that means I'll be alone. My kids will be gone, my wife will be gone, and I'll be all alone. Even worse, I'll be a failure, because I couldn't keep my family together. That's what a man is charged to do, right? Take care of the family and keep the family together.

My first child was born November 18, 1988. It was the middle of my third season with the 49ers, so we were in San Francisco at the time. What an amazing experience. When Karen's water broke, we got ready to go to the hospital. Nothing happened at first, so we figured we had plenty of time. After about an hour, though, she was in intense pain, and I started to panic, because we had a thirty-minute ride to the hospital. By the time we arrived, Karen was almost eight centimeters dilated. She was supposed to have a private room during her labor, but she was progressing so fast that they wheeled her right into the delivery room.

Like most couples, we went through childbirth classes so we'd be prepared for the big moment. We practiced breathing and concentrating—all that stuff that's supposed to help you deal with the pain. But let me tell you, that sucker didn't do a damn bit of good! Karen went in the delivery room and she just went crazy. She was howling, just hysterical. It was such an emotional thing that it made me cry. I'd never seen my wife in that kind of pain—shit, I'd never seen *anybody* in that kind of pain. I just wanted it to stop. Once, when I was holding her hand, trying to console her, she had a major-league contraction, man, and she dug her fingernails damn near through my hand. Broke the skin and everything. When she did that I started screaming. And she was screaming. We were both screaming together, at the top of our lungs: "*Aaaaaahhhhh!*" The doctor finally put his hand on my shoulder and said, "You know, you don't have to scream with her, Mr. Haley. That's not part of it."

I've never felt so helpless in my whole life. There was nothing I could do except be a cheerleader, and I even messed that up. I was rubbing Karen's back, stroking her forehead, kissing her, trying to be supportive . . . but knowing my place, too. I wanted to make sure that I stayed right near her face; I didn't want to go back to the other end, because I knew there would be all kinds of blood—that stuff makes me queasy. Funny, huh? A football player who can't stand the sight of blood? Well, that's the way it is sometimes, especially when the blood belongs to someone you love. Anyway, Karen started pushing, and after a while the doctor said, "Charles, come here! I see the head!" I was thinking, *Oh, boy . . . bad idea,* but I couldn't be a complete punk right there in the operating room, in front of all those people—not while my wife was suffering the way she was.

So I stood up, walked back to the other end of the table, and it was like *Wooooooo.* The whole room started spinning. And then . . . *Boom!* Down I went. All of a sudden there were doctors and nurses all around me, trying to lift me into a chair.

My baby was being born, my first child, and I was fainting. I didn't quite go all the way out, thank God, but it was close enough. Let me tell you, from then on I always stayed up at the head when my wife was giving birth. I never looked down again.

Princess Kay Haley is my daughter's name. We got along great right from the start. We just kicked it, me and her, like best friends. I loved spending time with her. I used to keep a baby bag with me all the time, because she went everywhere with me. I know a lot of men who won't change their kids' diapers; they think it's a woman's job. But I was changing Princess's diaper the day she was born. It was no big deal to me. I grew up changing diapers. There were always little kids around our house—neighbors' kids, cousins, nieces and nephews. I knew how to do that kind of stuff. And I kind of enjoyed it. It made me feel close to Princess. As soon as she was old enough to start crawling, she'd drag her little body across the floor and lay on top of me and fall asleep. Man, there's nothing like that—holding your child close, feeling her heart beating against yours. Like she's almost inside you.

My second child was born two years later. I told my wife, "Give me a boy and I'll give you anything you want." So, the day after Charles Junior was born, I was out at the Mercedes dealership, buying Karen a new car. I was walking on air, thinking, *Damn, this is what it's like to have a family. A daughter and a son. I must be the luckiest son of a bitch on*

Earth. I wanted to name him after me because I didn't know if we'd have any more kids. See, my wife and I—our philosophy is a little different when it comes to that. I like big families. That's the way I was raised. But Karen isn't into that. Two you can manage. Maybe three. But five? Then you just yell all the time. You can't manage five. You just try to survive.

Maybe it's best that we didn't have that big a family, though, because I kind of dropped the ball with my third child, Brianna. She was born January 15, 1994, the day before we beat the Packers in the second round of the NFC playoffs. My mind was not on my family at that time. My mind was on football. We went on to win the Super Bowl, and one week after the season I was in the hospital, undergoing back surgery for the first time. So I was in my own little world. That's no excuse; it's just an explanation. I was not as good a father to Brianna as I was to my first two children. We didn't bond right away. I try to spend a lot of time with Brianna now. I make an extra effort with her, because I have some catching up to do. For a while she treated me like a stranger, which broke my heart, because I had been so close to my other kids. But it was my fault. The first year or two of her life I wasn't at the house as much, playing with her the way I had played with Princess and C.J.

But I'm making up for lost time now. That's why I don't do a lot of stuff in the off-season: autograph shows, things like that. I want to spend time with my family. I take them back to Virginia, or I'll take them to Florida, or Hawaii. Someplace where we can do family stuff together, and where there are no distractions. I understand that you have to bond with your kids early; otherwise, when they get older, you're no help to them at all. If you don't earn their respect early, you're lost. I'm not going to let that happen.

———————

Maintaining a strong marriage is hard for anyone, and it's particularly difficult when you're a professional football player. There's so much tension in your life, so much anger. You hear a lot about domestic violence involving professional athletes. Well, it *is* a problem, and I'll tell you why. Too many men want to be king of the castle. Their wives aren't allowed to say anything. I respect my wife's space. I respect what she does with her life. That's the deal. A man has to respect his wife. You can't treat her badly just because she's a mother and a housewife and doesn't hold a regular job. You can't say, "You don't work, so you do what I tell you to do."

Unfortunately, that's the attitude a lot of players take. And if the woman has the guts to stand up to him, he feels he has the right to get physical. Then, if he gets caught, he starts whining about all the pressure he's under, and how his woman doesn't understand. Man, that is complete bullshit! Yeah, professional athletes live in a violent world, and we are under a lot of stress. But you know what? There's stress in every job. I've had enough lousy jobs to know that. You have to find a way to handle the stress, to channel it in another direction. I grew up watching men beat women. I've seen the effects of domestic violence. I've seen it all my life, and I'll be damned if

I'm going to be that way. There's no excuse for hitting a woman. *None!* If you're into excuses, you're not into reality. If a man can walk away from a situation on the football field, if he can show control in the heat of battle, then he can control himself at home.

The truth is, he doesn't want to control himself. He wants to control *her.* Instead of treating a woman as an individual, he treats her as property. I do not treat my wife as property. I treat her as my friend, my partner . . . my *wife.* I guess that's what keeps us on the up and up, keeps us out of trouble. That and the fact that my wife is highly educated and spent several years in the military. She's always reminding me, "You know, Charles, I can shoot the head out of a quarter at a hundred yards." So there's some intimidation there, too, which helps. Plus, I was raised by a skirt. I learned at an early age to respect the skirt. And I still do.

Marriage ain't easy, though. It's the only game I know where the playing field is 100 yards one day, 75 yards the next day, and 50 yards the day after that. The rules are always changing. Either you change right along with them, or you lose the game.

CHAPTER 8

Bootlegger's Boy

Jerry Jones didn't waste a lot of time. On March 30, 1994, one day after Jimmy Johnson announced his, uh . . . *resignation* . . . Barry Switzer became the new head coach of the Dallas Cowboys. Once again, I was pretty much in the dark. I didn't know anything about Barry. I didn't even know who he was. I didn't know anything about Oklahoma football, and the tradition he had built there. To tell you the truth, I didn't really care. I was just happy to see Jimmy leave.

I remember the day it happened there were a lot of meetings going on, people running all over the place, moving in and out of offices. Everyone was nervous—players and coaches. There had been talk about Jimmy getting canned, of course, but most people didn't think it would happen. After all, he'd won two straight Super Bowls. So there was a sense of shock when he left. Not for me, though. I was relieved, because if Jimmy had stayed, I probably would have been out of the picture. That's the truth. When I found out he was gone I thanked God, because I knew I'd have an opportunity to stay and try to win another Super Bowl. Jimmy was a great coach, but he had to be The Man. He couldn't tolerate anyone challenging his authority. And I had done that. He liked the way I played football, but he didn't like *me*. That's okay. I didn't like him either. If he had stayed in Dallas, I would have found a new home. No doubt about it.

That whole first year with Barry was like a learning experience. The first time I met him he was very friendly. He smiled a lot, shook my hand, talked about how thrilled he was to be the coach of the Dallas Cowboys. He was real upbeat. He told me if I ever wanted to know anything about him, I should just read his book. I wanted to be careful, but I sensed that he was a player's coach, someone you could mess with a little, so I decided to bust his balls.

"Hey, you want me to read your damn book," I said, "you better give me a copy."

Barry started laughing—he's got this big, deep, good-old-boy howl, and when he starts, he just fills a room. Right away I thought, *This might be kind of fun.*

The next day Barry gave me an autographed copy of *Bootlegger's Boy*, his autobiography. So I read it right away. Man, I'll tell you . . . it was pretty fucking deep. Barry's been through hell in his life, watching both his mother and father die. I don't know how you handle something like that.

I devoured the book, and I learned a lot about Barry. He grew up poor, in a black neighborhood. He knew tragedy, heartache, adversity. Before I ever played a game for Barry, *Bootlegger's Boy* made me realize that he's more than just a football coach; he's a good man. He cares about more than just winning and losing. He cares about the individual. Barry's life is a rags-to-riches story. He's got a little halo over his head or something; somebody's watching out for him.

The thing is, the money and the fame and all that? It hasn't affected him. Barry is one of those guys who can relate to his players—black and white. He doesn't have to put on airs just to satisfy one group or the other. He knows exactly how to work with everyone. After reading Barry's book and then seeing him with his family—he was always running off to watch his son play football, and his daughter was always hanging around camp—I couldn't help but like him. I wanted to play for him.

I wanted to help him win.

Barry had been out of football for a while; in fact, he hadn't coached since 1988, his last year at Oklahoma. So it wasn't like he had a ready staff to bring to the Cowboys. Instead, he just kept Jimmy's assistants and tried to let them do their jobs. Other than Barry, there weren't a lot of new faces around training camp, but things were definitely not the same. Everything about that year was different. Barry was much more laid-back than Jimmy, and his camp was a lot less physical. There wasn't the grind that you usually hear about. Barry was always walking around, joking and stuff. He didn't hold our feet to the fire. It was a big adjustment for some people. A lot of guys were used to having Jimmy ride them all the time. All of a sudden Barry was in there, trying to treat them like adults instead of children, expecting them to work hard simply because they were getting paid to work hard.

This was Barry's first experience working with professional athletes, and I think he expected them to behave like professionals. Unfortunately, it doesn't always work like that. Some people need a kick in the ass to get motivated; some people don't. That goes for the assistant coaches, too. Barry was hands-off. He didn't assert himself right away; he let the assistant coaches do most of the work.

We were all trying to change gears at the same time; it was bound to be a little rough. For some reason, though, a lot of people—coaches, players, fans, the media—thought it would be a smooth transition. They figured, *Barry Switzer's coming in as the new coach, but he's got most of the same players and assistants. All he has to do is leave the system in place and the Cowboys will win another Super Bowl.* But it didn't work that way. You see, Barry had a lot of knowledge about the game, a lot of wisdom and experience. And for some reason, he was reluctant to share it. At least for a while. He's a great guy and a great coach, but he's not a disciplinarian. He doesn't believe in jumping on guys, cussing them out, and he took heat for that. There were a couple times that first year when I even got mad at Barry, because we'd lose a close game and afterward Barry would come into the locker room and say, "God damn, that was exciting!" Then he'd walk around with tears in his eyes, hugging guys, shouting, "I love this game and I love all you fuckers!"

That took some getting used to, because a lot of people think it's some kind of submission to behave that way. I'll admit that it made me uncomfortable at first, and that there have been times when Barry and I have gone around a little bit. But I'll tell you, if I had to choose somebody to get on my back—if I had to choose between Barry Switzer and most of the other coaches I've had—I'd choose Barry, because he's a real human being. I respect him.

I didn't know what to expect from the Cowboys as a team in 1994. Barry had replaced Jimmy. We'd lost a few players on defense: Kenny Norton and defensive tackles Jimmie Jones and Tony Casillas. We were still a very talented team, but there were question marks. Including my own health. I'd recovered quickly from back surgery, and I felt reasonably strong and fit for the first time in two years. At the start of camp, though, I pulled a calf muscle, so I wasn't practicing much. It was frustrating. By the end of August, I couldn't wait for the season to begin. The Cowboys had traded for me largely because of my reputation as the best pass rusher in the game. But in '93 I'd recorded only four sacks. I had an excuse, of course—I was hurt—but still . . . *four sacks?* It was an embarrassing number, the lowest of my career, and I was determined to make amends.

We opened the season in Pittsburgh, against the Steelers. It was a good test. The Steelers were a tough, young team. They'd made it to the AFC playoffs the year before; they had one of the league's top running backs in Barry Foster, and a good quarterback in Neil O'Donnell. Before the game Barry Switzer came up to me in the locker room, looked me right in the eye, and said, "You know, you get paid a lot of money to do what you do. I've heard a lot about it and I've seen it on film. But I haven't seen it on the field. Today . . . I want to see it for real."

He saw it all right—the real fucking deal. A lot of people were predicting that Pittsburgh would run all over us because we had lost so many players. But we came out smoking. Emmitt rushed for 171 yards, Troy completed twenty-one of thirty-two passes for 245 yards and one touchdown, and Chris Boniol kicked four field goals. We cruised, 26–9. The best part, though, was our defense. We held the Steelers to 126 yards of total offense. Incredible! We were in O'Donnell's face all afternoon, sacked him nine times! I had four sacks myself, equaling my entire total for the '93 season.

I'll tell you, I was on air that day, man. My body felt great: lean, fast, strong. Like a kid again. It was gonna be a good season. I just knew it.

The next week was almost as good. We beat the Houston

Oilers, 20–17, for bragging rights in the state of Texas. Not only did I have one and a half sacks, but I also intercepted a pass for the second time in my career. Two games, two victories. And for me, five and a half sacks and one interception. Not a bad way to start the year.

We won eight of our first nine games before losing to the 49ers in San Francisco in the middle of November. But we bounced right back with three straight victories to run our record to 11–2. On Thanksgiving Day we beat the Packers, 42–31. I had six tackles and one sack, and received a game ball. The next week I had three sacks and five tackles as we clinched the NFC East title with a 31–19 win over the Eagles. Again I received a game ball.

We finished the regular season with a 13–3 record, good enough for another NFC East title and a bye in the first round of the playoffs. On January 8, 1995, we played the Packers again—and again we won. This time it wasn't even close: 35–9. For the third consecutive year we'd made it to the NFC Championship Game. And for the third consecutive year our opponent would be . . . the San Francisco 49ers.

The 49ers had a hell of a team when we beat them in the '94 title game, and now they were even better. Carmen Policy and Eddie D. had opened their wallets in a big way and gone after some of best free agents available. One of the first players they signed was Kenny Norton. Later on they added Bart

Oates, who won two Super Bowl rings as a center with the New York Giants; Ricky Jackson, a Pro Bowl linebacker who had been in the league for fourteen years; Richard Dent, a defensive end for the Chicago Bears who was MVP of the 1986 Super Bowl; and Charles Mann, a defensive lineman who had helped the Washington Redskins win a Super Bowl in '92. With the exception of Kenny Norton, these guys were all past their prime; but they could still play. Most important of all, they were winners. When you get to the playoffs, that's what you need: people who know how to win. And the 49ers, like the Cowboys, had a lineup *full* of players who knew a little something about winning.

They also had Deion Sanders—*Prime Time!*—who hadn't won anything yet . . . except the respect of just about everybody in the league. Deion was one of the game's best cornerbacks when he wasn't playing baseball, and he, too, had been signed as a free agent early in the '94 season. Up to that point he'd spent his entire pro career playing for a shitty team, the Falcons, and now he wanted a ring. So he took a salary cut and signed with the 49ers. With Prime in the secondary, the Niners weren't just a good team; they were a *great* team. And this time they'd be playing at home.

For the first eight minutes of the NFC title game, we looked like we didn't even belong on the same field with the 49ers. It had rained hard, so the turf at Candlestick Park had turned to mud. That threw us off a little—we were used to a fast track in Dallas—but the 49ers just rolled with it. On the third play of the game Eric Davis picked off one of Troy's passes and ran it back 44 yards for a touchdown. A few minutes later Davis stripped Michael Irvin. That set up a 29-yard TD pass from Steve Young to Ricky Watters. I was stunned. We kept fucking up and they kept taking advantage of it. And it wasn't over yet. The next time I looked up the 49ers were kicking off and Kevin Williams was fumbling the ball! Pretty soon the Niners were in the end zone again.

21–0!

And we were barely halfway through the first quarter.

We made a game out of it in the second half. Troy hung in there, kept firing away. Midway through the fourth quarter he hit Michael Irvin with a 10-yard TD pass to make it 38–28, and a few minutes later we had the ball again. That's when all hell broke loose. On second-and-10 from the San Francisco 43, Troy tried to hook up with Michael again. He tossed a bomb. Michael and Deion ended up fighting for the ball near the goal line. There was a lot of contact—it looked like pass interference—but no flag. Barry went fucking nuts, ran right out onto the field and bumped the referee. Well . . . there were plenty of flags after that. Unsportsmanlike conduct—*on the coach!* That penalty was a killer, because we might have had an opportunity to battle back. Instead we wound up with third-and-25 from our own 42-yard line.

We didn't score another point. There would be no *three-peat.* The final score was 38–28, and the thing I remember most is that Steve Young had a great game. His numbers weren't anything special—13-for-29, 155 yards, two touch-downs—but I thought he was fucking heroic. He ran the ball extremely well, he took a pounding, and he just kept going. Steve was named the league's MVP that year, and I can't say he didn't deserve the award. He showed me on that day that he really is one of the league's top-notch quarterbacks. I still don't like him, and I'll always remember what an asshole he was to Joe Montana. But you have to respect those who can and those who do. And on that day, Steve Young *did*.

Barry took the loss well, the way he usually does. He walked into the locker room, gathered everyone around, and said, "The two best teams in the NFC were playing here, and the best team won today." He didn't harp on it. That's the way Barry is. He shoots straight bullets and leaves it at that.

Still, there was criticism after that loss. Plenty of it. Expectations are always high in Dallas, and they were really high this time. We had the best talent, the highest-paid players, and we were still young. Everything was in order. We were supposed to win another Super Bowl—and we could have. But we didn't get it done. The fans, as far as I could tell, seemed to understand that we had given our best effort. When I'd go out and meet them they'd just smile, say, "Better luck next year," or "Go get the 49ers!" They didn't sit around going, "Yo, why y'all fumblin' up the ball?" and shit like that.

Most of the heat, as usual, came from the media, and it focused on Barry. He was criticized for not being enough of a disciplinarian, for not taking charge. People have to understand, though, that football players are grown men. These are not little kids. They're going to behave the way they want to behave. It's not Barry's responsibility to follow them around with a shotgun all day. Personally, I think he did a great job his first year. He was under a ton of pressure, coaching an NFL team for the first time, everyone expecting another Super Bowl title. The team had to grow and get to know Barry. It took time. He took the collar off the guys and let them breathe a little bit. He let them enjoy football again. A lot of the players on this team hadn't enjoyed the game for a while, because Jimmy Johnson didn't let them enjoy it. Instead of feeling like you were in a pressure cooker, waiting for Jimmy to blow his steam, being a Cowboy was fun again. Jimmy was into threats and intimidation. Barry was not. And because he failed to win a Super Bowl with a bunch of Jimmy's players, some people felt he wasn't up to the job. I don't understand that. Why take a man's kindness and call it weakness? By the end of that season Barry had my respect. We'd had our bad moments, and we'd have more in the future—shit, I've had bad moments with almost everyone—but I like him. He gave me a chance to screw up. He said, "Look, you know what you have to do. You know what you're supposed to do. Now go out and do it."

That's my kind of coach.

———

A word about retirement: Never say never.

I'm an emotional man. When I play football, I put everything I have into each game: heart, body, mind. Sometimes, in the aftermath of the battle, I say things that I wish I hadn't said. But when you're completely spent—when you're physically and emotionally exhausted—the words come pouring out of you.

After we lost to the 49ers I announced my retirement from professional football. I told my teammates first, in the locker room at Candlestick Park, moments after the game. Then I told the media. I didn't feel like answering questions about the game; I didn't feel like talking about football or playing football. I'd had one of the best seasons of my career—twelve and a half sacks, sixty-eight tackles, a fourth trip to the Pro Bowl—but it wasn't enough. I've never played football for individual glory. To me, it's about winning. I'd done my share of winning during my nine years in the NFL. I had four Super Bowl rings. At the time, I was thirty-one years old. I'd had a great career. I'd been beaten up a little, but I still had a chance to walk away with my back and legs and head in working order, which is more than a lot of guys can say. The money was nice, but I could survive without it.

So, in that moment, after a hard loss in the Candlestick mud, I was sure I'd never play another football game. "The bottom line," I told the reporters hanging around my locker, "is that this is my last year playing football. It's over. There's no need to ask me any questions about what could have been or should have been . . . football is no longer in my system."

Complete bullshit, of course, though I meant it at the time. A week later I was back in Honolulu, playing in the Pro Bowl, and by the middle of February I realized that football was not out of my system at all. In fact, football still fueled my system.

I wanted to keep playing. I *needed* to keep playing. And the Cowboys wanted me back. In March I agreed to play at least one more season. In July I renegotiated my contract: four years, $12 million, including a $3 million signing bonus.

Naturally I got beat up by the media after that. I was accused of pulling a power play—of "faking" a retirement in order to extort more money from the Cowboys. Nothing could be further from the truth. If I had wanted to use money as a ploy, then I wouldn't have said I was going to retire. That's not my style. I would have walked into Jerry Jones's office and said, "Pay more or I won't play."

But I wanted to play. And the Cowboys wanted me to play. My only stipulation was that they agree to make the team stronger, that they do exactly what the 49ers had done: Find a few new players who could help us get back to the Super Bowl. They said they would. So I agreed to return. At the time, I really thought I would last another four years. I still had the desire. I had the spirit and the knowledge. What I didn't have was the body.

I just didn't know it yet.

Charles in Charge, Part V
THEY'RE PAYING HIM HOW MUCH?

It's okay to be confident when you come into the NFL. In fact, it's necessary for survival. But you have to know when to keep your mouth shut. A rookie should do his job and go home. That's it. If other people want to talk about you, build you up . . . fine. Just don't fan the damn fire. Let the media take care of that nonsense. You shouldn't be talking about what you're going to do, whose job you're going to take, whose butt you're going to whip. You have to remember: There are a lot of dogs out there, and they take this shit very personally.

I've seen a few players come into the league with bloated résumés and big mouths. Almost all of them have had very short careers. Brian Bosworth was a good example. He came into the league in 1987, after he played at Oklahoma. He was supposed to be one of the best linebackers in college football, and a surefire NFL star. But he never had a chance. He strolled into camp a millionaire, with a stupid Mohawk haircut, a smirk on his face, and a bad-ass attitude. Trouble was, he couldn't back it up. He had no game. Not only that, guys were going after him like you wouldn't believe. They weren't just trying to hurt him—they wanted to maim that fucker. A lot of veteran players hated him just because he went from being a college player to having all these endorsements and everything. They were trying to kill him on every play. Each guard on both sides of the center would come off the ball looking for him; and then the tackles would go after him, too. When I was with the 49ers people used to talk about how they were going to get Bosworth, how they wanted to see him in pain. It was like he had a price on his head or something.

Bosworth only lasted a few years. He just couldn't live up to his image—not with that kind of hate coming at him every week.

Tony Mandarich was another overrated player, maybe the most overrated player I've ever seen. They talked about how he was supposed to be the greatest offensive lineman in history, the best thing since water, man. And I have to admit, when I saw films of him in college, he looked like an unholy fucking terror, just throwing people all over the place.

The media hyped Mandarich like crazy. When he was still in college, he appeared on the cover of *Sports*

Illustrated, naked from the waist up. He was an incredible physical specimen—a little too incredible, I thought. The guy weighed 300 pounds, but supposedly he could run the 40 in 4.5 or 4.6. Sorry, but that shit doesn't happen naturally.

I'm not saying Tony Mandarich was using steroids. I just know it was a rumor. There were rumors about a whole lot of guys. The league used to send people around to talk about steroid use, and they'd tell us how to look for the signs. I'd usually just tune them out, go to sleep. Doesn't matter to me if a guy's using or not—I still have to beat him. Why the hell should I waste my time looking at his neck, or trying to see if he's got pimples coming out his ass? Either way, I still have to face him. And anyway, the steroid users eventually screw up. They either test positive or they get hurt. Or, worse, they get off the juice and become . . . *ordinary.* I've noticed there aren't nearly as many cut-up players in the league today—you know, with the superhero bodies. Now you see more fat guys. I don't mean just fleshy. I mean big, fat guys, with that belly hanging over the belt, going *"Hey-Hey-Hey!"* Like Fat Albert.

I'm not sure what the story was with Mandarich. I only know that when I finally played against him, he was garbage. He couldn't pass block worth two cents; he could only run block a little bit. It just seemed to me like he didn't have a clue. Mentally, he was lost. And physically, well . . . I don't know what happened. He sure as hell didn't seem very strong or quick—nothing like the player I saw on film when he was in college. There was a lot of talk about how he was hit with all these tests and had to go off the steroids to avoid getting caught. I don't know. I do know, though, that the NFL is no joke, and he was getting his butt wiped.

Players treated Mandarich like a punk, just like they did Bosworth. They wanted to teach him a lesson. I sit back now, in retrospect, and think, *Why did we do that? It was cruel.* But when the league presents young players as super athletes, and pays them an extraordinary amount of money, they're asking for trouble. These players get thrown into deep water. And if they don't know how to swim with the sharks—right away—they're going to get hurt.

There's no room in the NFL for pretenders.

CHAPTER 9

Playing with Pain

Unless you're on the field, you can't really comprehend the violence of professional football. It is a brutal, unforgiving game, and you have to be a little bit insane to want to play it.

I came to that realization when I drew special teams duty during my rookie year with the 49ers. Players who really want to make the team can score points with the coaching staff by throwing their bodies around on punt and kickoff coverage. It's like a rite of passage for everyone except the bonus babies, which I definitely was not. Look good on the special teams and you can guarantee yourself a place on the roster, because every team needs a guy with brass balls.

It's suicidal, of course, but I didn't care. I was going to do whatever they wanted me to do. So, during the first few preseason games, I'd come flying down the field on kickoffs, running right through the wedge . . . utterly fucking fearless. I'd run through eleven people if I had to—whatever it took. In a game against New Orleans, though, I got flattened. I was sprinting down the field the way I always did, numb with rage, when someone blindsided me. I left the ground for an instant—I mean, I was flying sideways; then I got hit again, by someone else. And then again . . . and again. My eyes were rolling back in my head, but somehow I still made the tackle. I don't know how, because I was knocked silly. When I came off the field everybody was slapping me on the back, congratulating me, telling me that they heard Bill Walsh say, "That Haley's a tough son of a bitch, isn't he?"

Very few people make a career out of playing on special teams, and I sure as hell didn't want to be one of them. Not after that. Fortunately, I had proved myself to Bill and the other coaches. They took me off special teams duty and told me to concentrate on defense. But I'd had my wake-up call. This wasn't college ball anymore—this was a man's game.

———

Television does not do the game justice. On TV you can't hear a guy whimpering and moaning after he's been practically knocked unconscious. You can't see the fear in his eyes. You can't hear ligaments popping, shoulders separating. As a player, you remember the sounds as clearly as the sights. I think people watch us on TV and presume we're protected, just because we're wearing all that gear. A lot of times, though, players will alter their equipment, especially the wide receivers and running backs. Instead of legitimate knee pads they'll use a little piece of foam—just enough to look good, so that the refs don't throw them out of the game. And they might not even bother with thigh pads. On the defensive line we use really small thigh pads. I'm constantly messing up my thighs, but if I use big thigh pads, I won't be able to move as well. It's a tradeoff.

The people who take the most abuse are the people you can't see: the interior defensive linemen. They have the worst job. They're constantly getting cut, double-teamed, and twisted up by the offensive linemen. Most of those guys only last a few years, and when they come out of the league they're all busted up: bad knees, broken hands, hurting all over the place.

Football players don't age like normal human beings. I've had an eleven-year career, which is an eternity for a professional football player. I'm thirty-three years old, but I feel like I have the body of a sixty-year-old man. It isn't just attitude that determines how you feel. I wish it was, because I'm a pretty chipper guy most of the time; I have a lot of energy. But my body doesn't respond the way it used to. I can't go out and play basketball. I can't run the way I used to. I can't even wrestle with my kids. I've had three knee surgeries, two shoulder surgeries, and three back surgeries. Eight operations in eleven seasons. As you can imagine, this old body of mine is pretty much torn up.

Recovery is different for an athlete. Nine times out of ten, when a professional football player comes back after surgery, he comes back months before he's supposed to come back, because he's terrified of losing his job. Athletes are used to dealing with pain, so they don't give us much of a break. They wheel us out of the operating room and right into physical therapy. We plow through rehabilitation at twice the speed of a normal person. We take painkillers and injections. We lie to ourselves and we let others lie to us.

Anything to get back on the field.

There is an unspoken code that rules life in the NFL: *Deal with it.* You're not supposed to get hurt. But, of course, you do get hurt. *Everyone* gets hurt. The ability to play with pain determines whether or not you'll make it as a professional football player. You start the season in good health, feeling strong, fast, invincible. Then you sprain an ankle, twist your back, break a finger. You take so many hits that your ears start ringing. By the fourteenth week of the season every bone in your body aches, every muscle is bruised. The great players find a way to get past the pain, usually with a little pharmacological help; and the teams that win championships have a lot of great players. As Jimmy Johnson used to say, "You can't let the grind get to the mind."

No one tells you any of this when you're a naive rookie in your first week of training camp. But you pick up on it soon enough. You watch. You learn. You see what the older guys are doing and you follow their lead. That's the way legacies are established. It's the way traditions are handed down. And it's the way the NFL works. If you make a certain amount of money, you are expected to play with pain.

It takes a pretty serious injury to keep a highly paid player out of a game. Instead, for a lot of guys, treatment becomes cyclical. You get your knee drained on Monday, take a cortisone shot on Tuesday to get the joint to calm down a little, then take an injection to numb it on game day. Then you repeat the whole cycle the next week.

The fact is, you're always going to be hurting; it's just a matter of how much. Even if you don't have a serious injury, something will be bothering you. Maybe your ribs are bruised. Maybe you have turf toe. That's a really common injury. I'm lucky—I've never had it. But from what I hear it's really painful. Your toe turns black and you can barely walk. A lot of guys take injections for turf toe. Then they're good as new . . . for a few hours, anyway.

The needle is magical shit, man. It does wonders. It hurts like hell when it goes in, burns like a son of a bitch. But that's when you know you're at the heart of the pain, when the doctor squeezes the novocaine through the syringe. The pain intensifies for a few seconds, and then it eases up. When the needle comes out, it's like the pressure is relieved and the pain is sucked out through that hole. Fifteen to twenty minutes later the medicine kicks in and you're ready to play. Your feet may be numb—or your fingers, or your ribs, whatever—but you learn to accept the side effects. The important thing is this: The pain just . . . *disappears!*

The fans, of course, don't even realize what's going on. You see players getting hurt and limping off the field into the locker room, looking like they're half dead. Then, a few minutes later, they come sprinting out of the locker room, all fired up, pumping their fists, ready to play. And the crowd stands up and starts cheering, going crazy. What the hell is that all about? You think that guy's a wimp when he's out on the field, and all of a sudden he goes into the locker room and becomes Superman? Uh-uh. It's the needle. It's modern-day science that helps us make it through.

In some ways, the needle is the football player's best friend. It allows him to face the pain, to deal with having his body torn up. The sad part is, it allows him to take more chances. It allows him to play when he shouldn't be playing. On each team there are probably three or four guys taking a needle on any given Sunday. No one talks about it very much; it's just expected. The "dos and don'ts" have been bred into you as a football player: You *do* take the needle and you *don't* complain. The burden is entirely on the player. You can say no. But if you say no you'll be labeled a "punk." They'll say, "He's scared of playing with pain." Your teammates lose respect for you and the coaches start looking at the guy below you on the depth chart. Resting an injury may be good for your body, but it doesn't do much for your career. On a team like the Cowboys, where expectations are extraordinarily high, and there's so much competition, no one gets away with not taking an injection. Basically, the doctors will say, "Here, I can numb

Does this look like the face of a future All-Pro defensive end? I was a real cutup as a kid. But I sure was cute, wasn't I?

Danny Wilmer was an assistant coach at James Madison when he came to visit me in Gladys, Va., in 1982. I was a late bloomer, so there wasn't a lot of competition for my services. I respected Coach Wilmer, and I was happy to sign a letter of intent with JMU.

I had some of the best times of my life at James Madison University. This is when I was pledging at Alpha Phi Alpha fraternity.

It was at James Madison University that I really learned the game of football. Aggressive defensive plays such as this one (I'm number 87) helped me become a Division I-AA All-American.

Parents' Day at James Madison in the fall of 1986—one of the proudest
moments of my college career. That's my mom, Virginia, and my dad,
George, walking out onto the field with me.

Challace McMillin was there on the day I was inducted into the James Madison Hall of Fame. That was important to me. Coach McMillin was a good coach and a good man. I learned a lot from him.

The 49ers locker room was like a morgue; everyone was so serious.

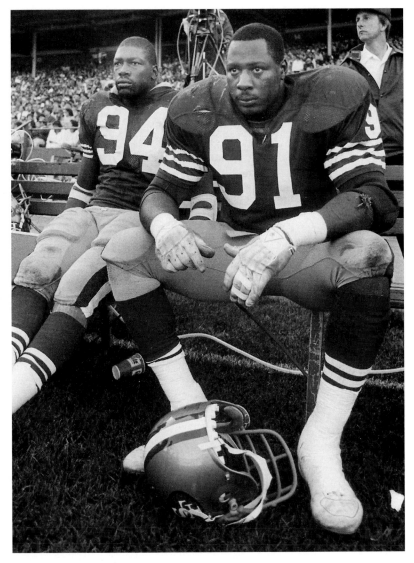

My rookie year with the 49ers (sitting next to defensive end Larry Roberts). What a learning experience. I tried to work hard and keep my mouth shut.

Me and the Magic Man—Joe Montana. I've never seen a better quarterback: Joe could do it all.

A postgame meeting in 1991—my last season with the 49ers. That's me in the back, addressing the team. By this time I was accustomed to speaking my mind, even if I was half-naked.

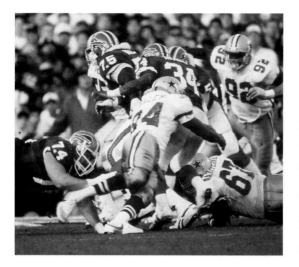

Putting a hit on Buffalo running back Thurman Thomas (34) in Super Bowl XXVII. The Bills were no match for the Cowboys. We rolled to a 52–17 victory.

Visiting the White House never gets old. This was my third trip, in March of 1993, after the Cowboys beat the Buffalo Bills in Super Bowl XXVII. That's Jimmy Johnson and Jerry Jones flanking President Clinton. I'm behind Jerry.

At the Cowboys training camp in the summer of 1993. Karen is five and a half months pregnant.

Halloween is a big night around our house. That's C.J., left, and Princess with Karen, in 1993.

My mom, Virginia Haley, feeding two-week-old
Brianna on Super Bowl morning in Atlanta in 1994.

On January 6, 1994, I celebrated my thirtieth birthday with two of the
people I love the most: my son, C.J., and my big brother, George.

The whole family in 1995 (including my mother) at the children's Christmas party given every year by the Cowboys.

December 13, 1995

Mr. Charles Haley
Dallas, Texas

Dear Charles:

I heard the news about your recent back surgery,
and I wanted to add my voice to that of your
many other fans in wishing you a full and speedy
recovery. I look forward to enjoying more of the
exciting plays that have characterized your career
and made you one of the best in the league.

I enjoyed the talk we had when the team came to
the White House in 1993, and I hope you'll come
by again when you're in the area.

Sincerely,

Bill Clinton

When this letter arrived from the White House, I was in complete shock.
The president of the United States actually took the time to wish me well.
As you can imagine, I'm now a big fan of Bill Clinton.

Taking a breather during a Cowboys game.

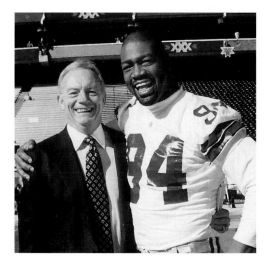

That's me with Cowboys owner Jerry Jones. A lot of people don't like Jerry, but I've always gotten along with him just fine. Jerry's like me—he likes to win.

John Madden is one of my favorite people. I love the guy! He's great for the game of football. And he's always been a big supporter of mine. As far as I'm concerned, being named to the All-Madden team is a greater honor than making All-Pro.

Me with Ronnie Lott. Ronnie may be the best safety who's ever played the game. He made me realize there's more to the game than brute strength or speed.

Karen and I like to take the kids on a nice family vacation every year during the off-season. This is Sea World, in Florida. That's Charles Jr. on my right, Brianna on my left, and Princess looking over my shoulder.

Relaxing with Karen. She's the perfect woman for me—smart, tough, caring. I don't know what I'd do without her.

I've played in five Pro Bowls, and I've enjoyed each one. The game itself is actually fairly low-key—no one wants to get hurt in a game that really doesn't mean anything. But you also want to look good when you're sharing the field with the best players in the NFL.

that." Then you look in their eyes, and the eyes of the coaches, and you realize there's no such thing as saying "No."

For me, obviously, the biggest problem has been my back. Bruised ribs, separated shoulders, torn knee cartilage . . . they all hurt. But there's nothing like a herniated disk. Thank God for "pain management." It's kept me on the field. Every couple weeks I'd go down to the clinic and get an injection. I went there so often the last three years that the receptionists stopped getting excited to see me. I wasn't a celebrity anymore. It wasn't like, *Holy shit! Here comes a Cowboy!* Nope. I was just another guy with a bad back.

As I mentioned earlier, there's no counseling involved in this program. No mind games designed to help you deal with the pain. The treatment is strictly physical. I'd walk in and they'd have a table waiting for me. I'd take off my clothes, lay down, and they'd start an intravenous drip. Then the doctor would tell me to relax, which was impossible. Pretty soon, though, he'd shoot something into the IV and I'd be off to la-la land.

You can see the equipment, because it's all out on a table, and you can hear them talking to you. But you don't really feel anything. It's like you're floating . . . dreaming. It's actually kind of peaceful. Prime Time had a back problem, too. He went with me a couple times, and he thought it was great. He really loved it. He just laid there like a little baby, smiling, eyes closed, going, "Damn, dog! This feels so good right now." I was laughing, man, because at first Deion wanted to just walk in, take his injection, and go home. He didn't want the IV. But I told him, "Hey, the IV is the best part. Anyway, they can't go in without giving you something to knock you out, not with that kind of needle."

That's no lie, either. It's a long motherfucker of a needle—long enough to go all the way down to the spine. It's a scary process, but I have to admit it works. You can't drive afterward, of course, because you're all drugged up. So either my wife or one of the trainers would have to take me. I'd lay there for two or three hours, feeling really peaceful. Then, around 10:00 that night, when the medication wore off, it would hurt like hell. The next day and the next night the pain would intensify around the area where the needle went in. So it would hurt even more for a while. But around the third or fourth day it would start to feel better. By Friday the pain would be completely gone and I could go out and practice. On Sunday I'd be ready to play.

And on Monday I'd be in agony, counting the days until I could get another round of "pain management."

By the middle of the season, a lot of players need help to get ready for the game and to get through the game. You'll see them in the locker room, with their little plastic bags. You never know what's in there, but they've got them. All you know is, they go to the bathroom a whole bunch of times, and they take their bags with them. Guys will take all kinds of shit:

pills to make them breathe better; pills to give them energy. Anything for an edge. It's all mental. They need something, so they take a little speed and they swear it helps. They'll say, "Man, I feel like I can run all day." The really scary thing, though, is that they'll mix this shit. They say they know what they're doing. Maybe they do. Or maybe the guy who's taking them knows what he's doing. But then other players borrow his shit, and they start messing around with it, and who knows what happens. Some of it's just over-the-counter stuff, but even that scares me. I don't even drink coffee, which is what some guys do: they guzzle quarts of the stuff, get a real caffeine rush before going out on the field. Same effect as speed.

I've never been into any of that crap. I don't need any help getting psyched up to play football. When it comes to dealing with pain, though, we all need a little assistance. I've taken injections before games; I've taken injections during games. And over the past few years, as my back has deteriorated, I've taken to chewing Vicodin, a painkiller, like it's candy. Brett Favre, the Packers quarterback, said he developed an addiction to Vicodin during the 1995 season. I can see how that could happen. It's not that hard to get Vicodin. Players need it, doctors prescribe it. There are clear limits on how much they're allowed to prescribe, of course, but for any resourceful player, that's only a minor hurdle. If you can't get enough from the team doctor, you can get it from other players. And if you're seeing your own personal physician for an injury, you can double up. For example, I could go to one of the Cowboys' team physicians and ask him for some Vicodin. When he gives it to me, he's unaware that my own doctor has already given me a prescription for both Percodan and Vicodin. It's not difficult to build up a nice stash.

I started taking Vicodin when I first hurt my back. After a few months I wasn't getting much relief from the usual dosage. They'd tell me, "Take two every four hours." So guess what? I took four every two hours. Then I started going to pain management and I got it under control. I didn't have to take Vicodin very often during the week. On game day, though, I'd take two to four Vicodin, plus a couple Percodan. That would cut the pain a little, allow me to get through the day. The only problem was, I couldn't go to sleep afterward. I'd be wired. Early in the 1996 season I hurt my back so bad that I took two Percodan before going to bed, in addition to the Percodan and Vicodin I had taken before the game. Thirty minutes later my back was still killing me, so I took two more. An hour later I was sitting up in bed, sweating like a pig, with my heart racing, practically jumping out of my chest. I started to panic.

"I think I'm having a heart attack!" I yelled to my wife.

Karen jumped up, scared to death. "What did you take?! How much?!"

When I told her, she wanted to call an ambulance. But I knew that was bad news. I could just imagine the scene: EMTs pulling up in front of the house, sirens blaring, lights flashing; me being carried out on a stretcher. My picture would be on the front page of the *Dallas Morning News* the next morning, my mouth hanging open, tubes sticking out of my arms, my wife and kids crying. And above the photo, some sick head-line:

Drug Overdose KO's Cowboy!

No, thank you.

I tried to relax, get it under control. After a while, my heart stopped pounding. I stopped sweating. The anxiety went away.

I looked at Karen and smiled.

"If that ever happens again, and I die . . . don't tell anyone what happened. Just drag my sorry ass out in the street and run over me a couple times."

Most of the time it's not that dramatic. In fact, I usually sleep pretty well the night of a game. We all go out afterward, get a big meal, have a few beers, and then go home. I take a pain pill on top of all that and pass right out. Works like a charm.

The next day, though, the locker room looks like a scene out of *Night of the Living Dead*. Everybody comes staggering in—limping, shuffling, lurching all over the place, grunting and groaning like they've been hit by sniper fire. I usually spend two or three hours in a hot whirlpool, trying to let the pain seep out of my body. I come out looking like a prune, but I feel a lot better. Then I get a rubdown, or whatever kind of treatment I need. The trainers, man . . . they're the heroes of the locker room. They do a great job catering to the players' needs. I don't know what we'd do without them. They'll stay around as long as you need them; they'll even bring treatment to your home. They go out of their way to make sure you're ready to play.

Of course, that is their job. In Dallas, it's rare for a trainer to suggest that someone shouldn't play, just as it's rare for a doctor to tell you not to play. One of the things that bothers me is when you ask the doctor, point blank, "Should I play?" And he returns the question: "Well, do you *think* you can play?" Except in the most extreme circumstances, the team physician will not give a direct answer to that question. He puts the decision on the player's shoulders. Team doctors are afraid to take a stand and say, "No. You should not play." Even with my back, as bad it got in 1995 and 1996, the Cowboys would not take a stand. They never recommended that I not play, even though it was clear that I had a serious injury.

In fairness to the 49ers, I have to admit that it was somewhat different in San Francisco; they took a more cautious approach. Lyndsey McClean, the head trainer, would examine a player, and if he felt the injury was severe enough, he'd recommend that the player sit out. And the team physicians were more likely to recommend surgery. In Dallas, it seems like there's more of an emphasis on getting the player out on the field—at any cost.

The team doctor has a tough job. I know that. He's supposed to look out for the players, but he's also working for the team. He has to report to the owner, and the owner wants to see his best players on the field. Regardless of who's paying their salary, though, they're still liable. They're medical doctors giving a medical opinion. If a guy has a minor injury, they should say, "Okay, I'll push him out there." But if a guy has an injury that really requires rest, they should say, "I'm holding him back."

Doctors have to be more honest with players. If they don't think a player should play, then say, "Look, why don't you take a week off?" Don't try to reverse it and make it the player's decision. Of course the player is going to try to get out there: he fears for his job. He knows he's expected to play, so he plays. Shit, I'm not the one who went to medical school to become a doctor. That's why I have to ask the question: *Should . . . I . . . play?*

Sometimes it seems like the only way a doctor will tell you not to play is if you have an injury that requires immediate surgery. And I do mean *immediate.* A few years ago Mark Tuinei, one of the Cowboys' offensive linemen, played most of the season with a torn anterior cruciate ligament, an injury generally considered to be about the worst thing that can happen to a football player. Not only did he play, but he practiced! That's one of the things that really gets to me. Not only are you expected to play in games when you're hurt—they want you to practice, too. How can they expect a guy to live with that pain all week, and then go out there and play at a high level on Sunday? It's crazy.

Jimmy Smith, a wide receiver for the Cowboys in '92, came

down with appendicitis during training camp. The doctors told him to take some Pepto Bismol and get back out on the field. Said he'd be fine. The coaches made him practice and everything. Well, Jimmy kept getting worse; he lost about twenty pounds, could barely stand up, but no one would believe he was really sick. They kept telling him he had indigestion. Fucking incredible! The man had appendicitis and they were prescribing Pepto Bismol. He damn near died before they started taking him seriously. And the really sad thing was, when he couldn't play anymore, they didn't want to pay the man. He had to go to arbitration to get the rest of his money. That's why I always tell anyone with a bad injury, "Go see another doctor." It's the only way you can be sure you'll get an honest diagnosis.

Even head injuries are treated casually. Got a concussion? Too bad. Twenty-four hours, man, and your ass is back out there. Concussions are as common as turf toe in the NFL. We're constantly being told not to lead with our helmets when we tackle. *"See what you hit,"* the coaches tell us. That way, supposedly, you're less likely to get a concussion or a neck injury. But it doesn't really matter. If you've got a 220-pound running back colliding with a 250-pound linebacker, at full speed, there's going to be some damage. Your head's going to snap back. A lot of guys get dinged, get pinched nerves. Stingers, we call them. Your arms go numb for a minute. You see stars. It's no big deal. The trainer rubs your shoulders a little bit and you get right back out on the field.

Violence is a dirty word in the NFL, so the league takes a contradictory stance on the subject. We're told, *"Don't use your helmets when you tackle. We don't care about big hits."* But then you see the games on television and you get a completely different message. What's the first thing you see when any NFL show comes on the air? The biggest, nastiest, meanest hits they can find. Bodies flying. Bones breaking. Because that's what people want to see. That's what sells the game. And yet, every year they change the rules about hitting. Supposedly, the NFL is trying to protect its players. If you look closely, though, you'll notice that the rules are designed to protect only the high-profile players: specifically, quarterbacks. The quarterbacks are the stars. They make a ton of money, and the league needs to protect its investment. So you have all these stupid rules to make sure the quarterback doesn't even get his fucking uniform dirty, let alone get hurt. They want to make it so all you have to do is tag the quarterback and he's down.

To which I say . . . *"Bullshit!"* If you're a pass rusher and you're doing your job, you don't have time to see where you're putting your hands or your head. You're fighting off two, three, four people to get to the quarterback, you're all worked up, you're playing hard, and they want to dictate where your head is? You just want to get the guy down.

I play at a high level on every play. God knows, if I get a

chance, I'm going after the quarterback. They want to fine me? Go ahead. I don't give a damn. I'm not going to try to go one hundred miles an hour and then come to a dead stop just to protect the guy I'm supposed to hit. They want me to pull up? I'll pull up, all right . . . right after I knock him on his ass. I'll hit the quarterback any way I can, because that's the way the game is supposed to be played. It's crazy, man. If you go out there worrying about where to put your head, or whether you're going to be fined for hitting the quarterback, you become a timid player. And timid players are the most likely to get hurt.

I love football, despite all the pain and suffering. But I've sacrificed enough of my body for this game. I'm not going to make it easy for someone to take me out.

Charles in Charge, Part VI
MAN'S BEST FRIEND

It's a cliché, right—the big, tough football player with the big, tough dog? But it's also real. I love dogs, and so do most football players. Emmitt Smith has a couple of huge dogs. Nate Newton, one of the Cowboys' offensive linemen, is a pit bull guy. He's got, like, five or six of them. They're all over the place. Tony Tolbert's got one of those big Alaskan dogs, a husky. And a bunch of other guys on the Cowboys have rottweilers.

Why? I'm not sure. I think it's just a release, a way to give love and be loved unconditionally. That's the main reason. A dog can bring out another side of a person. If I come straight home after a game or a practice, I don't hang out with my family right away. I'll either play on the computer for a while, or, more likely, I'll take my dog for a walk. His name is Midnight. He's a Doberman pinscher. I didn't get him because he's supposed to be mean or nasty or whatever (as a matter of fact, he's a real sweet dog). It's just that I grew up with dogs, and for some reason I became fascinated with pinschers. I had a bunch of miniature pinschers when I was playing in San Francisco, but every one got killed within six to eight months. It was heartbreaking. Just when I thought I had them trained, they'd run out into the street and get hit by a car. In 1989, on the day we won the NFC championship, my wife was home with the baby and somebody rang the doorbell. Karen answered the door and our dog slipped out. He sprinted right out into traffic. The son of a bitch who hit him didn't even stop—just leaned on the horn and kept right on going.

I can't understand how anyone could do something like that. I mean, dogs are just beautiful. They show you straight love, man. Sometimes they don't come when you call them, and sometimes they'll tear up the yard. But they'll also sit there and let you rub them and play with them for hours. It makes you feel like a kid again. It makes you forget the problems you have—at least for a little while. I take Midnight with me all over the place. I take him to Valley Ranch, the Cowboys' practice facility, when I'm getting treatment or something. Guys come over and play with him, pet him. He doesn't bother anyone.

Something happens when I'm with my dog. A calm comes over me. I love my kids, but they always want to jump on me, play with me, and sometimes my body just can't take it. I'm too messed up. And, of course, then they're disappointed. My wife gets pissed at me, too.

Everybody gets pissed—except the dog. I can always take the dog for a walk. I can talk to him and know that he's not going to talk back and tell me all the things I didn't do or shouldn't do. He'll just listen. He may not understand a fucking word, but he'll listen. That's what makes him really great.

I'll admit that there's probably an image thing involved with a lot of athletes; after all, you never see a football player walking a poodle or a cocker spaniel. But I didn't get a Doberman because I wanted an attack dog or anything like that. I just wanted a smart dog, a dog that would challenge me. I could have gotten a rottweiler. They're easy. You train them once and it's over. A lot of the big, tough dogs are like that. You train them once and they never forget it. Dobermans are strong-willed, though. You have to stay on them, keep working with them. But they're loyal. And they're beautiful.

A lot of football players would never admit it, but the real reason they have dogs is because they need companionship. You see a lot of single guys with dogs, and I think it's because they're lonely. It's scary out there, man. You don't know who you're bringing home. Sometimes it's safer to just hang out with the dog. I mean, the dog doesn't have to sleep in bed with you or anything, but he can sit with you while you're watching TV. He can lie on the floor at the foot of the bed while you sleep. And you know he won't hurt you, like some other people you might bring into your bedroom. In fact, he'll protect you.

The truth of the matter is this: Professional athletes are under a lot of pressure, and they use different tools to relieve the stress. I know Troy Aikman is a big fish guy; he collects tropical fish. They say if you sit and watch them it helps you relax, calm down.

Whatever works. For me, it's dogs. The problem is, my dog loves people. He'll run right over to anyone he sees. He won't jump on them or hurt them, but he'll be social. And in my neighborhood, that's like a crime or something. Anybody else's dog can get loose and run up onto your front steps and it's no big deal; nobody freaks out. But if my dog gets out, people start calling the cops, calling my house frantically, like the dog's going to eat their kids or something.

I find that really insulting. If you treat my dog like that . . . you're treating *me* like that.

CHAPTER 10

Front Page Blues

As long as I've been playing football, I've hated the media. Even when I was in high school. I used to read newspaper accounts of games that I had played in, and most of them sucked. They were badly written, inaccurate, dumb. It always seemed like the reporter knew nothing about football. I was sixteen the first time I turned down a request for an interview, and I've been turning down most of them ever since.

My opinion of the media hasn't changed over the years; if anything, I'm even more critical. Reporters aren't interested in the truth. They're interested in selling newspapers and boosting their television ratings. They don't care who they hurt or how they hurt them. It seems like the job of the media is not simply to report the news, but to dig up every bad thing a person has done in his entire life. I understand that sometimes you have to show the bad with the good—I'm not naive. But

I think when reporters are so committed to showing negativity and being as controversial as possible, just so they can sell newspapers and make a name for themselves, then something is wrong. Something is getting lost in the translation. You never see stories about players working with kids, doing charity work, or hanging out with their families—human interest stuff. I guess no one is interested in that stuff anymore. It's dirt or nothing.

I don't understand why the media has to pry into a player's personal life. What does that have to do with anything? Unless you're a convicted felon, what's the point? Shouldn't some things be off limits? Shouldn't there be some privacy, even for a celebrity? What motivates a reporter to follow a player to a bar and keep track of how much he drinks? Just so he can write, *"On Tuesday night, so-and-so was out getting drunk"*? If a player tests positive for drug use, or gets caught driving drunk, or something like that, then you have a story. Otherwise, it's irrelevant. I think what players do off the field is their business. When you start poking into someone's personal life—into family matters—then it's an invasion of privacy.

Unfortunately, once you achieve celebrity status, you apparently forfeit your right to privacy. Your entire life becomes fair game. The media has the right to say anything about you, print anything about you. I always tell people, "God, I love playing football. I love being a football player and I love the money that goes with it. But the notoriety and all that other stuff? You can keep it." That's why I'm always chasing reporters away from my locker, saying, "Hey, there's forty-five or fifty other guys in this locker room. Please . . . build them up. Leave me alone."

It doesn't seem to matter, though. I hardly ever talk to the media; and yet, an awful lot of stories have been written about me. I'm usually portrayed as some sort of Dr. Jekyll and Mr. Hyde—you know, a man with two personalities, always on the verge of erupting like a volcano. The truth is, everyone has a dark side, but with me, it's like I'm subhuman or something. I don't get it. A writer talks to me for five minutes (or doesn't talk to me at all, which only proves my point—they don't even need my help) and then feels he has the right to paraphrase my entire life. Or to psychoanalyze me. I don't need that. I don't want that.

To me, it's a matter of trust. I don't expect reporters to cover shit up—I know that's not their job. But I do expect them to be competent. And in my experience, that's usually not the case. When I was in high school and college I'd read all these stupid stories about the football team, and I'd wonder where they got their information. It was so far off base. When I was with the 49ers, the coverage became much more intense. But it wasn't any better. I'd hear the beat writers interviewing players, and the next day I'd read the stories, and it was like everything had been paraphrased or taken out of context. I've read some amazing interviews in my career: brain-dead players sounding like geniuses, using words they couldn't even think of pronouncing. That shit makes me laugh. Or two separate stories with different versions of the same quote. How the hell does that happen?

Sometimes it seems like a reporter's job is to write half-truths; to take the tiniest bit of truth and take it through any door that's convenient, just so he'll have a story. I recognized that early in my career, so I've shied away from the whole process. When I was in San Francisco it shouldn't have been a problem. We had so many prima donnas in that locker room —guys starving to have a camera in their face—that I should have been left alone. But someone would always say, "Why don't you talk to Charles. He's the defensive leader." And then —*Boom!*—they're swarming all over my locker, like locusts. Picking at me, feeding off me.

Reporters are relentless. They'll keep coming back to you, even when you've already told them that you don't have anything to say. They'll come over and bug you, shove a tape recorder in your face. That's another thing I hate, man. You come out of the shower and you're trying to put your clothes on, and all these microphones and cameras converge on your locker. If you've never been in an NFL locker room, you can't imagine what it's like, how annoying it is. They don't even give you a chance to get dressed. You're supposed to stand there completely naked, dripping wet, while they ask questions. I know reporters are working under deadline pressure, but . . . give me a break. Can't we at least have a few minutes to get dressed?

The lack of privacy can lead to problems. When I was in San Francisco I was accused of flashing a female reporter— which did not happen. I came out of the shower and she was there, standing at my locker, and I didn't feel like talking to her. So I cussed her out—while I was naked. But you know what? I had just cussed out a male reporter, too. I wasn't doing any interviews that day, but I guess she figured she had brass balls, because she came at me anyway. And I blew up.

This incident occurred at around the same time that a female reporter from Boston accused a couple of New England Patriots players of sexual harassment. So everyone was very sensitive about the issue of women reporters in the locker room. My personal stance on it is this: Women who are credible reporters have every right to be in the locker room. But there has to be some privacy, too. The players should have a chance to shower and put on their underwear or a bathrobe before women come in and stroll through the locker room. If that creates an unfair advantage for male reporters, then simply keep the locker room closed to all reporters until the players are dressed. Once the reporters are in the locker room, though, I'm not going to show any favoritism. If I'm going to yell at a male reporter, and tell him I don't feel like talking, then I should be able to yell at a female reporter, too. The ball bounces both ways. If a woman wants to be just as aggressive as a male beat writer—just as *rude*—then she shouldn't expect me to treat her delicately.

This particular reporter did. And the front office people with the 49ers got very upset about the whole incident. They were worried about their image. They were concerned that what happened in New England would happen in San Francisco. They'd get skewered by the media and there would be some kind of revolt at the ticket office. So they asked me to apologize. I was dead set against the idea at first, because I hadn't done anything wrong. But upper management made it quite clear to me that I'd better do what they wanted. So I swallowed my pride and apologized.

To this day I feel bad about giving in. That entire incident was bullshit. It was all about appearances and being politically correct. I don't care about any of that. When it comes to reporters, I treat everybody the same. I'm an equal opportunity prick. If a writer dogs me, I'll never talk to him—or her—again.

I've been accused of being more accessible to black writers, but that's not true. I'll joke around with some of the black reporters, because they'll come in and talk about some bullshit they heard on a black radio station or something like that. We share a culture, so that makes it easier for us to just kick it a little. But I don't give the black reporters any more stories than I give the white reporters. Anyone is welcome to come on over and shoot the breeze with me, just fool around, as long as they don't try to get me to talk about football. But white reporters tend to be more intimidated in the locker room. They stand in a corner and watch the black reporters come up to my locker and make small talk. And then the white reporters get envious and start saying, "See, he only gives interviews to black writers." Check with any of the black reporters, though. They'll tell you the truth: I'm not giving them shit. And I'll cuss out any writer: black, white, male, female.

Believe it or not, I do understand the role of the media. I know they serve a purpose. I know that if it weren't for the media, our games would not be publicized. And if our games weren't publicized, we wouldn't make the kind of money we make. I just wish the media would concentrate on football and stay out of the players' personal lives. And I wish they were better at their jobs. For example, why aren't beat writers more creative? Why don't they show some guts once in a while? Reporters come into the locker room and they just listen to each other's questions, instead of trying to dig and find out what's really going on. Why the offense is not clicking. Why the defense sucks. Instead, they all just play it safe: *"We're not going to talk about this guy because he's the star quarterback; and we can't burn this guy because he's the star running back."* Place the blame wherever it should be placed. Just put the facts out there.

But it doesn't work that way. Reporters have certain people they protect. That's how they get inside information. It's not always accurate, but it makes for good copy. There are players on the Cowboys who will sell out their teammates in a minute, and just about all of the coaches will do it. If a coach wants to ridicule a player, he can just call up one of his boys in the media and spoon-feed him a negative story. Then the reporter writes the story, citing "anonymous sources." How gutless is that? Overall I think Dallas is a better organization than

San Francisco. But I'll say this: The 49ers knew how to keep things in-house. If a coach had something to say about the way you were playing, he'd call you in and tell you to your face. With the Cowboys, it's just a bunch of ex-college coaches who don't know how to handle professional football players. We're grown men, not children. Be honest with us. Don't go running to the media.

It's like, we'll have a team meeting, something very private, and the next day the subject of the meeting is in the newspaper. Well, one of three things has happened: A player said something, a coach said something, or the meeting room was bugged.

A player who cooperates, who knows how to play the game, generally won't get pounded by the media. Unless, of course, he gets caught in a compromising position off the field. Then the media swoops in and tears him apart. That's the way it works. You can be a good boy, say all the right things, cultivate your image, but if you fuck up even once— you're history.

It's true what they say about the pen being mightier than the sword, because the media can, and will, ruin your life. It blows my mind that reporters have that kind of power, especially since most of them aren't even qualified to cover football. If I were an editor, one of the first things I'd do is hire people who know something about the sports they're supposed to cover, rather than just getting Joe Blow off the street. I'd get guys who can not only write, but who played football and have some understanding of the skill involved in the game. If I had more respect for the people who cover our sport, I wouldn't be so hesitant to cooperate with them. I'm sure other players feel the same way. So many sportswriters are ignorant, especially the columnists. What a job they have: just sit back in an armchair, surrounded by bulletproof glass, writing whatever they want to write. As far as I can tell, a columnist has one function: to stir up trouble, to be as controversial as possible. Even if he's a complete fucking idiot, he gets to air his views publicly, for thousands of readers. I don't know how those guys sleep at night.

If I had the chance to do it all over again, would I do anything differently? Maybe. I like Rich Dalrymple, the Cowboys director of public relations. He's a good man, and he's taken the time to work with me on some of this stuff. He's made me realize that there are ways to deal with the media in a professional manner—without selling your soul. But it's hard for me. I'm too honest. I'm too candid. Players today already know the drill when they come into the league. They know all the little things you're supposed to say and not say. They have all the quotes and clichés memorized, so when someone sticks a microphone in front of them, they just flip a switch . . . and out comes the bullshit.

I've never been able to do that, and it's probably cost me. After I won my fifth Super Bowl ring, you had to really dig to find any stories about it. If it had been anybody else, it would have been front page news, plastered everywhere. But I have the kind of personality that reporters love to hate. This was a chance for them to get even. That's okay. If they're going to punish me or dislike me—without even knowing me—just because I choose not to talk to them, then fine. I can't stop them, and I'm not going to try.

You should be rewarded for your accomplishments on the field, not for the amount of effort you put into promoting yourself off the field. I've been told that my lack of cooperation in this area might one day cost me a chance to get into the Pro Football Hall of Fame, because sportswriters do the voting. That's out of my hands. If I get in, great. It would be nice, because it would mean that I was pretty good at what I did. I'd be placed alongside some of the game's greatest players, which is quite an accomplishment. But it's never been a dream of mine to make the Hall of Fame. I play football because I love it, and because it's what I get paid to do. I'm not going to change who I am just so the media will like me better and elect me to the Hall of Fame. If I can't get in based on the things I do on the field—if my work is not good enough—then I shouldn't be in there anyway.

I should be judged on my work, not on my personality. No matter where I've played, I've achieved excellence. I've always played hard, I've always been a winner. And I have the respect of everyone I've ever played with. To me, that's the most important thing.

———

Despite my disdain for the media, and my reluctance to play according to the rules, I must admit that I have a certain degree of admiration for people who know how to use it to their advantage. The system generally rewards those who conform and punishes those who rebel. That's why I applaud anyone who is able to turn the system on its ear. Deion Sanders is a great example of that. Prime Time is a showman. When he was with Atlanta, I used to love watching him. I didn't even care if he scored a touchdown or not—I knew we'd find a way to win, because we were a better team. But just to watch him, man . . . the way he could take a crowd from booing to shutting up, or make them get on their feet. I've always respected the shit out of him for that. God gave Deion incredible athletic talent, but he's not one of those superstars who doesn't use it. He comes out and works hard all the time. I'm just happy he's a Cowboy now.

The only thing that bothers me about Prime is that I hope someday he learns to accept being the best cornerback in the league and stops trying to be Superman. Forget about playing wide receiver and running back punts. I've seen him on long drives, sucking air sometimes. This man is in top shape, but nobody can sustain that energy level. I guess that's why he does it, though—to prove a point. He wants the glory. He wants to be *Prime Time*!

It's impossible to resent Deion's success, because he's earned it. He came into the league with style and attitude, but he had the talent to back it up. Deion is something special; he's a once-in-a-lifetime athlete. He knows who he is, he's determined, he has the will, and he has the God-given athletic ability to make it all happen. In other words, he has the whole package. It's the selfish part of me that wants him to concentrate on defense. I understand that he has to be his own man; he has to make his own decisions. Deion is always looking for new challenges, new opportunities. As long as he can get the job done, it's hard to be too critical.

I don't even mind him playing baseball again. In fact, I'd rather see him play baseball than wide receiver. No one—not even Prime Time—can successfully play offense and defense in the NFL for any length of time. Eventually, you're going to get seriously hurt. But baseball? What's the worst thing that could happen? You pull a hamstring . . . get a little tendinitis in the elbow. It's not exactly like having someone trying to take your head off when you're running a crossing pattern, is it? Deion is Deion, though. He's going to do what he wants to do. And he's going to make a shitload of money doing it.

You know who else I like: Dennis Rodman. Now there's a guy who's beating those suckers at their own game. I don't know whether he's homosexual or bisexual or heterosexual or whatever. And I don't care. All I know is, he's playing the game by his own rules, and he's winning. I hear people sit there and say, "Oh, God, Dennis Rodman is so disgusting!" But he's a performer. Am I not right? He's a professional. He's just like an actor playing a role. Of course, he also happens to be one hell of a basketball player. Like Prime Time, he's perfected his sport. He can rebound the ball like no one else in the NBA. Every team wants a guy like Dennis Rodman, someone to do the dirty work, to get the ball so that the Michael

Jordans of the world can score. If he couldn't back up his act with a legitimate game, then it would be different. Then I'd have zero respect for him. You have to have the game. If you've got nothing to bring to the table and leave there as collateral, guess what? People are going to say, *"More assets, please!"*

To do what Dennis has done—to become bigger than life—you need a gimmick *and* a game. He's always had the game, right? He was always "The Worm," even when he was in Detroit. He was always the guy getting the rebound, working his ass off. Then all of a sudden he covered himself with tattoos, dyed his hair, got a nose ring, and started acting all crazy and shit, and suddenly everybody wanted to know more about him. That's brilliant, if you can pull it off. It's not for me, but it works for Dennis. People love what he does. He's learned how to make money off the court—on his own terms. I think that's great. And he's done it without sacrificing his reputation as an athlete.

The only question I have about Dennis is how much he's faking the funk. Does he really have that quick, fiery temper, or is that just part of the act? Because if it's real, sooner or later it'll get his ass in big trouble. Like when he kicked a cameraman during the 1996–97 season. What was that about? So there was a cameraman on the court. Big deal. The man was just doing his job. If it weren't for the cameras, Dennis Rodman wouldn't be a millionaire. He has to know that. He can't have it both ways.

Charles in Charge, Part VII
THE DOMINO EFFECT

You want inside news about a football team? Ask the trainers. They know what's going on. They know the mood of the team, right down to the deepest, darkest secret.

Players spend a ton of time in the training room, hanging out in the whirlpool, getting rubdowns, getting taped. Guys spill their guts in there. They talk about wives, girlfriends, kids, injuries, money . . . *everything.* Sometimes the players try to whisper, and the trainers pretend not to hear, but they do. They don't miss anything.

Of course, no one really minds, because the trainers have such an important job. There's a bond between the player and trainer. Without those guys, a lot of the time we wouldn't be able to get out on the field. I know that better than anyone. That's why I try to do special things for the training staff. They don't make a whole lot of money, even though they work their asses off. So when I get a contract from Nike or Converse or whatever, I'll pass along the freebies: jackets, shoes . . . stuff like that.

I'll buy workout suits and equipment for them. I'll do *favors* for them. Shit, I do all kinds of stuff for our trainers. Not because I'm looking for special treatment; I just want them to know that I think the job they do is invaluable. I appreciate their work.

What I don't appreciate is being slapped in the face, which is what happened one day in 1995. Kevin O'Neill was the head trainer then. He was a big guy, with a big butt and wide hips, and I used to pick on him a little bit. When he walked through the locker room I'd say, "Watch out for wide right!" You know, like it says on the back of a truck: WIDE RIGHT TURNS. But I was just joking around. That's the way I am. I'm a ball-buster. I don't mean anything by it. Anyway, Kevin used to give it to me pretty good, too. I didn't mind. I thought we got along just fine. Before he left the Cowboys, though, we got in a little scuffle, and I had to hit his ass a couple times.

It was the middle of the season. I was playing dominoes with Emmitt Smith, which is something I often did. I love dominoes. In fact, I'm crazy about the game. My wife even bought me a special set engraved with the words *Charles: World Champion* because I played dominoes all the time and always bragged about beating everybody. After Emmitt and I finished playing, we went to a meeting. I left the dominoes on the table, and

Emmitt left some other stuff: keys, papers, things like that.

Now, what I didn't realize was that Kevin was doing a slow boil about people messing up his training room. He liked things nice and neat, and apparently people had been leaving stuff all over the place. A few days earlier someone had supposedly eaten some food back there and left some garbage on the floor, which made Kevin furious. So I guess he was ready to snap. But so was I. In fact, I'm always on the edge. All I need is an excuse to lose my temper. And Kevin gave it to me.

When I returned from the meeting my dominoes were gone. But Emmitt's stuff was still on the table. I was seething. I marched up to Kevin and said, "Where the fuck are my dominoes?"

"I threw them in the trash," he said. "People are always leaving their garbage back here. I'm tired of it."

Now, at that point I had to do something. I couldn't just let him get away with it. All my life people have tried to make an example out of me, so other guys will say, *"Don't worry, they'll go after Charles, but they won't go after you."* That's bullshit. I had never left anything in the training room. I had always been extremely respectful of the training room and the men who work there. He did not have to throw my dominoes away, especially if he didn't have the balls to touch Emmitt's stuff. Nothing against Emmitt, but that's the star system at work again, and it's wrong. So I went back into the training room and just ripped the fucking place apart. I threw stuff all over the floor. There was tape everywhere, sticking to the walls, hanging from the ceiling. After I was through I looked Kevin in the eye and said, "How's that shit feel, big man?"

You can say it was trivial and I should have just said, *"Okay, what the fuck. They're just dominoes."* But they were *my* dominoes, and they were important to me. By throwing them away he was attacking me personally. So we went toe-to-toe, and I hit that fucker. You bet your ass I did. He's a big son of a bitch, and he wanted to fight. Afterward he tried to get me suspended, which didn't work. But he did get to me. That was one of those days when I felt like quitting. My back was killing me, I was playing in pain every day, and now I had to deal with the trainer shitting on me. So I just walked out and went home.

Later on Barry Switzer came to the house and told me to stop acting like a damn child. He told me to grow up. Everyone said I handled the situation the wrong way, but what recourse did I have? If I didn't act then, the moment was gone. The chance to right a wrong would have been lost. I was not going to let him get away with that. But what really hurt was the feeling of betrayal. I would have done anything for those guys. I would have given any of the trainers, including Kevin O'Neill, the shirt off my back.

CHAPTER 11

Lord of the Rings

1995

I announced my retirement from professional football on December 4, 1995. I had been unable to finish the Redskins game—a game we lost, 24–17, by the way—and a magnetic resonance imaging test the next morning confirmed my worst fears: another herniated disk. I needed back surgery . . . *again!*

I wasn't lying when I said I was through; I wasn't crying wolf. At the time I was taking Vicodin just about every day, and it wasn't putting a dent in the pain. I couldn't stand up straight. I couldn't sleep. I couldn't move without excruciating pain. I'll tell you, it nearly broke my spirit. After the Washington game I was in the locker room, crying uncontrollably, and my teammates were looking at me, like, *"God damn!*

What's wrong with him?" Everyone was used to me just saying, "I'm hurt—now give me a fucking needle and let's go." But not now. This pain made a grown man—a man who thinks he's pretty tough—break down and cry. It was the first time in my life that I just couldn't handle the pain. Usually I put it in different places, hide it until the game is over. Then I deal with it. But now it was right there . . . staring me in the face.

The idea of playing any more football was ridiculous. It was time to heal, to move on with my life.

That blast of logic lasted less than twenty-four hours. By Tuesday morning I was on a flight to Los Angeles to meet with Dr. Watkins. Before leaving I told a few reporters that I had changed my mind. Dr. Watkins was a good man, a good surgeon, and he'd fix me up. Maybe I was through for the season (then again, maybe not), but I'd be back next year. That's how much I loved the game, how addicted I was: I couldn't even stay retired for one full day.

On December 6 I endured my second microscopic lumbar diskectomy. Since I'd been through it before, I knew what to expect. Dr. Watkins removed a protruding fragment of disk between the fourth and fifth lumbar vertebrae on the left side of my spine. Surgery isn't a big deal to most football players, and it wasn't particularly frightening to me. I'd always handled anesthesia pretty well and recovered quickly. My concern was whether I'd be able to get back on the field before the season was over. In my heart, I knew that's what I wanted. We had a chance for another Super Bowl title, and I fully intended to be part of that experience.

When it comes to surgery, my biggest problem is that I heal too fast. Or, at least, that I trick myself into thinking I'm healed. I'm stubborn. I want to play, even when my body isn't ready to play. This time was no different. I stayed in Los Angeles for four or five days and then started my rehabilitation program right away. I looked at the calendar: six weeks until the Super Bowl. Plenty of time.

I missed the last three regular season games: a loss to Philadelphia and victories over the New York Giants and Arizona Cardinals. We drew a bye in the first round of the playoffs and then pounded the Eagles 30–17. That put us in the NFC Championship Game for the fourth consecutive year. On January 8, six days before we were to meet the Packers, Dr. Watkins gave me the green light to play. He didn't tell me I *should* play—he simply gave me permission. There was a distinct possibility that I could aggravate the injury. If that happened I might or might not have long-term problems; but I would certainly miss the Super Bowl.

It was a tough decision. The Packers were a good, young team coached by Mike Holmgren, who was the 49ers' quarterbacks coach when I was in San Francisco. Mike had done a great job with Brett Favre, helped him become one of the best QBs in the league. We were playing well, too, and I was pretty sure we'd win even if I didn't play. Still, there was this nagging doubt, this little voice telling me, *"Yeah, but what if you lose? You wanna be standin' on the sideline in street clothes . . . like a chump?"*

I decided I'd try to come back for the NFC title game. The day before the game, though, I changed my mind. Here's what happened. I was down on the field, practicing in pads for only the second time since my surgery. I was stiff, sore, and more than a little anxious. All of a sudden Dave Campo came up to me and said, "How do you feel? You ready to play?" Well, goddammit! He knew how I felt, and he knew I was *trying* to get ready to play. All he had to do was stay the hell out of my face. At that point I didn't want to deal with the coaching staff at all. Hell, if it weren't for some of the assistant coaches pressuring me to get out there and practice in training camp, after I'd told everyone that my back was hurting, I might not have needed surgery in the first place.

Anyway, that tipped the scales. Physically, I knew I was not ready to play. Christ, it had only been five weeks since my surgery! And now I was pissed off, too. I was in no mood to risk serious injury for that motherfucker Campo. So I did the math again: *The Cowboys might need me now to win this game, but my back is still hurt; if I play in this game, I probably won't be able to play in the Super Bowl.*

I knew it was going to be a one-game shot, so I added and subtracted, and here's what I came up with: *I'll wait.*

If the opponent had been San Francisco, it would have been a different story. The 49ers had beaten us the last two times we played: in the 1994 NFC Championship Game and in a regular season game in '95. I don't know how that happened. We used to say, "The hell with the 49ers!" and then go out and kick ass. But now they had us all psyched out. I blame that on the coaches. They'd start talking about individual players: *"Here's what we have to do to stop Jerry Rice; here's how we stop Steve Young."* That's not how you prepare for a team. It means you're scared. When you just play a team, you don't know names. They're not individuals, people to fear. They're just a bunch of guys. Somehow, in two years, we went from *spanking* the 49ers to acting like we didn't belong on the same field with them. We'd kick the shit out of other teams, but when we played the 49ers, it was like we were one of the worst teams in the league. We couldn't stop anything. In two games they'd scored seventy-six points against us. That's an embarrassment.

The players have to take responsibility for not getting the job done, of course. But in order for anything to change, for anything to happen, the man leading the damn boat has to have some guts. And Campo was leading the boat. I don't blame Barry. He's like a lot of head coaches: he moves from drill to drill, makes sure things are going smoothly, addresses the team once in a while. It's the coordinators and the position coaches who really run the offense and defense. They have to sell the dream to the players. Campo wasn't selling shit! Yeah, we were a good team, winning a lot of games and everything, but I still think we underachieved that year. We had all these assets—all these great players—and Campo would sit around thinking, *Everybody here is so stupid, I'm not even going to bother putting in any new defenses.* So we just had two or three simple defenses; we were relying solely on talent. The smart teams, like the 49ers, figured that out, and they picked us apart. They beat us up.

Fortunately, the Packers went down to San Francisco and beat the 49ers. That shocked me. But it also made me realize that I could probably get another week's rest. Even with our boring approach and our unimaginative coaches, we'd still beat the Packers. And that's exactly what happened, although it wasn't quite as easy as I thought it would be.

We needed two touchdowns in the fourth quarter to pull out a 38–27 victory. What I liked best about that game was watching my two boys, Tony Tolbert and Leon Lett. Tony played defensive end, opposite me, and he was having a really rough year. I mean, he was playing all right, but he was all messed up: two bad knees and a bad elbow, all of which would require surgery after the season. Against the Packers, though, Tony had two sacks and five tackles. *Outstanding!*

As for Leon, well, he was a terror: three tackles, one sack, even had an interception—the first of his career. Leon had been suspended for four games late in the season for violating the league's drug policy, and against Green Bay he played like he had something to prove. One of the Packers kept taunting him, and after a while Leon just lost it. He almost broke the guy's back, he hit him so hard; he took shit from no man that day. Made me proud.

We had two weeks to prepare for Super Bowl XXX against the Pittsburgh Steelers. The first week I tried to just rest and relax; I worked out a little on my own, went to team meetings, tried to get mentally prepared. I felt like I was making progress. My back was healing faster than expected, I was doing a little running, some light lifting. If God was smiling, I'd get through the Super Bowl without crippling myself for life. All I needed was a little luck.

For a few days, though, luck seemed to be in short supply. On Sunday, one week before the game, the team flew to Tempe, Arizona. Almost as soon as we arrived, I got sick. It might have been the flu; more likely, it was an infection. After the operation I noticed that one of the sutures was poking out of my skin; from what I understand, that can sometimes cause problems. Then again, maybe it was the good Lord trying to tell me to keep my sorry ass at the house and not go out there and play. Whatever the reason, I ended up flat on my back in my hotel room, sick as a damn dog. I had a fever, the sweats; I was sick to my stomach. I'd never been so sick in my life. The doctors gave me antibiotics and hooked me up to an IV to prevent dehydration, but I still didn't have the strength to get out of bed. I made it to a media session on Tuesday (only because we were required to be there and I would have been fined for skipping it—despite being ill) and staggered to the practice field on Wednesday. I couldn't do much, though. It was Saturday before I could keep any food down, and Sunday before I started to feel whole.

I'll tell you, man. It really sucked. I like to get out a little on Super Bowl week, enjoy the experience. This time I saw almost nothing but the walls of my hotel room, and half the time they were out of focus. My wife wouldn't even stay in the same room with me. She stayed next door with the kids so she wouldn't catch whatever it was that I had.

When my fever broke on Saturday, I felt more relieved than anything else. I could just imagine the shit I was going to have to take if I missed the Super Bowl because of the flu. Back surgery couldn't keep me down, but an upset stomach . . . ? I'd never hear the end of it. When I was lying in bed I was praying to God to make me feel better, because there was no way I was going to miss that game. The only way I wasn't going to play was if I died. As long as I was breathing I'd be in uniform, even if they had to wheel me out there. That's how bad I wanted to get my fifth Super Bowl ring. I can say I wanted to win it for Barry—despite our clashes, he's one of my favorite coaches, and I wanted people to get off his back—but that would be a damn lie. I wanted it for myself. I'd given a lot to the game over the years, and now I wanted to be selfish. No one else had ever won five Super Bowl rings. Hell, a lot of great players never even get a chance to play in a Super Bowl. This was a dream, a chance to accomplish something no one else had ever accomplished. Nothing was going to stand in my way.

I slept well Saturday night—so well that I didn't hear my

wake-up call. Security had to come and bang on my door. I flipped on the TV, watched cartoons for a little while, then took a shower and went downstairs for the pregame meal. The atmosphere was different than it normally is before a game. On Super Bowl Sunday, everyone is quiet—even me. In the dining room all you hear is the clinking of silverware. And the locker room is quiet as a church. Everyone realizes it's a big game; the stakes are higher. No one feels much like talking. I understand that, so I try to stay reserved. There's a lot of stress in the air, and I don't want anybody to use me as an excuse for not playing well. You know, *"Charles was jumping around, talking shit, bothering everyone, and that's why we lost."* On Super Bowl Sunday, I keep to myself. I let everyone do what they gotta do.

My back felt great during pregame warmups. I didn't let anybody hit me . . . until the very end. I knew I couldn't go out on the field without having taken a single lick in almost seven weeks. My body would have gone into shock. So, right at the end of warmups, I told Mark Tuinei to give me a shot. We were working on pass rushing toward the offensive tackle, and he hit me on the inside shoulder, a good smack that straightened me up, twisted my back a little. I stopped and waited for the pain to cut through me . . . but it never came! Not even a twinge. Mark smiled at me, gave me a pat on the helmet, and I thought, *Damn! Maybe I'm gonna have a good game after all.*

Before the game there was a special ceremony during which a bunch of former Super Bowl MVPs were introduced to the crowd. That was fun for me, because I knew a lot of those guys; I'd played with some of them, like Jerry Rice, Joe Montana. They came running out on the field, and as they went by I had a chance to holler at them, bust their nuts a little bit. And they'd turn back to me and yell, *"Go get 'em, man!"* or whatever. That was great, really pumped me up.

When the game began I was a little nervous. I can't deny that. I'd been away a long time. I'd had back surgery, the flu. In addition to my back, I was concerned about my conditioning. I started, of course. There was never any doubt about that. As long as I was capable of playing, I was going to be in the starting lineup. Still, I was afraid I'd get out there and be so winded after two plays that I'd have to leave the game.

I expected the Steelers to really come after me, treat me like a punk because I'd been laid up in the hospital and all. In fact, that's exactly what they should have done . . . but they didn't. Instead, they sat back, like they were scared or intimidated. You sense that kind of thing on the first play; it gave us an advantage right from the jump. So I just played hard, acted like my back didn't bother me a bit. I kept moving, tried to make sure they never put a big hit on me. And they never did. A lot of little ones, but nothing that was going to knock me out of the game. The thing is, if they had really gotten up my ass from the start, I would have had a long day. They made it easy.

To be honest, I thought Super Bowl XXX was a pretty dull

game. We got a lead and our offense went basic and boring, the way it always does. You know, just give the ball to Emmitt and let the defense protect the lead. Which we did, thanks to the fact that their quarterback, Neil O'Donnell, forgot who to throw the ball to—or who *not* to throw the ball to. He kept missing his own receivers and laying the ball in Larry Brown's hands. Larry got his first pick late in the third quarter. His return set up a one-yard TD run by Emmitt and gave us a 20–7 lead. But then the Steelers kicked a field goal and recovered an onside kick, which really pissed me off. We were all on the sideline talking about it. We knew they were going to kick short. They had nothing to lose. I remember thinking, *If they get it, it's gonna take the momentum away.* And that's exactly what happened. We went back out on the field and tried to hold the Steelers again. But we were tired—our defense played more than twenty-one minutes in the second half—and after twenty consecutive offensive plays the Steelers finally put the ball in the end zone. Now, with 6:36 remaining, our lead was down to three points, 20–17. At that moment I realized, *Shit! They could beat us.* Once you lose the momentum that late in a game, it almost never comes back.

And we never did get it back. We just got lucky. We went three-and-out on our next possession, giving the Steelers plenty of time to put together a game-winning drive. But with a little more than four minutes left, O'Donnell, under a heavy blitz, lost his aim again. His receiver broke one way, and O'Donnell threw in the other direction. I don't know who fucked up, and I don't really care. All I know is Larry Brown was right there waiting for it. He ran the ball back to the Pittsburgh six-yard line. Then Emmitt scored on a four-yard run to put the game away. The final score was 27–17.

Afterward, Larry was named the game's MVP and was given the Pete Rozelle trophy, which was nice, because he'd had a tough year. Early in the season his wife had given birth to a baby boy, but the child was born prematurely and died ten weeks later. Larry deserved to have something good happen in his life.

———————

Right before the end of the game I gave Barry a big hug. He was ecstatic, man. I'd never seen him so happy. It was like he was spitting in the face of all those people who said he was just riding Jimmy Johnson's coattails. This was his Super Bowl, his team. I was happy for him.

The locker room was crazy . . . pandemonium! Guys jumping around, crying, laughing, yelling, hugging. My back was hurting—had been hurting since halftime, in fact—but I took a couple Vicodin and that seemed to smooth it out. Some guys can barely control themselves after a Super Bowl win, but I'm usually pretty low-key. I never get very excited. That doesn't mean it's not important to me; I just don't like to show that much. All my emotion comes out during the game. Afterward, I'm kind of peaceful. I don't take a lot of pictures in the locker room or anything. I don't walk around with a video camera. I just sort of soak it all up with my mind. And then I move on.

It was nice to win my bet, though—the bet I had with Ronnie Lott. He said I was too old and beat up to get a sack in the Super Bowl. But he was wrong. I got to O'Donnell once. That gave me four and a half career Super Bowl sacks, more than any other player in NFL history. The bet was, if I got a sack, and we won, the next time I saw Ronnie I'd get to put on all five rings and pop him. Leave five knots with five diamonds on them right on his big motherfuckin' head. Of course, it was a safe bet for Ronnie, because he knew I'd never catch him with all five. Later, I saw him when I had two of the rings with me—I don't even know why—and I wanted to give him a smack. But he said, "Nope, five or nothing." Someday maybe I'll take all five of those rings and put them in a bag and pay a visit to Ronnie's house. Surprise the shit out of him.

Probably not, though. I owe him too much. Ronnie called me the night before the game and said, "Don't let the flu get you down. You have a job to do: go out there and kick some ass!" As long as I've known him he's done all the things that a friend is supposed to do. I love him to death.

As for the ring, it went right into a box, just like the others. I don't have to wear it. It's enough that I know it's there. It's something my kids can be proud of. You know: *Daddy didn't quit. Even when everything was really hard, Daddy never quit.* That's something no one can ever take away from me. They can take my rings, my house, my money . . . but they can't change history.

History doesn't lie.

Charles in Charge, Part VIII
YO, BUBBA!

One of the great things about playing for a championship football team is the perks. And one of coolest perks is meeting the president of the United States. I'm lucky. I've spent so much time in the White House over the last ten years that I almost feel like a cabinet member: *Charles Haley—Secretary of Football*. Has kind of a nice ring to it.

I realize that it's become something of a cliche for the president to meet the members of any team that wins a national championship. And the ceremony probably looks kind of trite to an outsider. Let me tell you, though, man—it's an incredible thrill, a great honor. I wish everyone got a chance to do it. For me, it never gets old.

The first time I went was in 1989, after the 49ers beat the Bengals in Super Bowl XXIII. The players were allowed to bring their wives on that trip, and Karen was really excited. After all, she was a military woman, so this was like going to heaven for her. They gave us a long tour of the White House and then brought us into a room and asked us to line up. The whole team was standing there: coaches, players, owners. We were all quiet and nervous. Then the president walked into the room. This was just a few weeks after George Bush had been inaugurated, and he didn't look terribly comfortable. He was polite—you know, he shook hands with everyone, moved down the line quickly, and then went about his business—but he seemed kind of quiet. Probably had a lot on his mind.

We visited the White House again the next year, and this time Bush was a little more relaxed. Still, he was nothing like Clinton. Bill is amazing. I met him in January of '93, after my first Super Bowl title with the Cowboys. We won again the next year, but Jerry Jones didn't take everybody—he only invited the Golden Crew: Jimmy Johnson, Emmitt, Troy, Michael. I did, however, get to go again in February of '96, after I won my fifth ring. Both times Clinton was incredibly charismatic. When he walked into the room he just took over. I'd heard he was a pretty big guy, but I didn't expect him to be quite so impressive.

The first time I started clowning around with him, making jokes, trying not to treat him like the president. I think that made Jimmy and Jerry nervous, but Clinton seemed to like it. In fact, there's something about him that makes you want to throw an arm around him and ask him if he'd like a beer. He's brilliant, you know? And he's a big, strong guy, with a firm handshake. He looks you straight in the eye and smiles, like he's thinking, *I can run the goddamn White House and come over here and beat your ass at football, too!* That's the way he carries himself. He has a certain air about him.

At the same time, he makes you feel at ease. I don't know how he does it. Al Gore was there, too. He's another big guy. A little short on charisma, though. Al needs to lighten up a little, take a lesson from Bill.

I can't help but be a Clinton fan. When I was about to have back surgery late in the 1995 season, I received an envelope from the White House. I was so shocked that I was afraid to open it—I thought maybe it was a prank or something. But it wasn't. Inside was a letter from the president, telling me how sorry he was about my back problems, and urging me to keep the faith. I couldn't believe it. A personal letter from Bill Clinton! That really lifted me up, man, because I was about to go under the knife and I was thinking I might never play football again. That letter was one of the reasons I was so determined to get back on the field. Six weeks later I was playing again, helping the Cowboys win another Super Bowl. And then I was back at the White House, shaking hands with Bill.

That was a kick. He took time to recognize me in his speech, and when he came down the line, I told him '96 was going to be a good year: He was going to get re-elected, and we'd win another Super Bowl. "See you back here next year," I said.

Unfortunately, I was only half right. Bill got the job done. The Cowboys didn't.

CHAPTER 12

Black and White

After the Super Bowl I flew to Honolulu for the 1996 Pro Bowl. I love the Pro Bowl. It's always in Hawaii, and it's a great little vacation after a long season. Somehow, though, this particular trip became a nightmare.

As usual, it was my mouth that got me in trouble. Lynn Swann, the former Pittsburgh Steelers wide receiver, who now works for ABC, grabbed me on the sideline and asked for an interview. I thought, *Why not? What harm can it do?* The next thing I knew, Lynn was asking me what I thought about the likelihood of Craig Boller replacing John Blake as the Cowboys defensive line coach. Blake had left the Cowboys to take a job at the University of Oklahoma, and Boller had been one of his assistants. I probably should have tried to be diplomatic, but I had never hidden my feelings about the coaching staff in the past, and I wasn't about to start now. I leaned into the microphone and spoke from the heart:

"I don't think the defensive coaches this year did a good job at all. If they stay in-house, that means we're not going to get better up front. They need to go out and get a qualified guy to come in here and teach some of these young guys, because the young guys are the future. But they'll probably stay in-house and keep somebody in there who is not really qualified to do the job."

Ooops . . . I'd done it again. That's the kind of thing that drives my wife crazy. She hears me spouting off on TV, or reads about one of my tirades in the newspaper, and she gets all pissed off. "Charles!" she'll say. "Can't you just keep your damn mouth shut?! Try this: *no comment!*"

Karen thinks I only talk to the media when I want to stir up trouble. Not true. Sometimes things just slip out. The fact is, I was being entirely honest in my assessment of our coaching staff. I honestly believed that we needed to look outside for someone to replace Blake. I wasn't trying to be hurtful or mean. It's just that I'm not good at sugarcoating my opinions. I'm honest. That's the way it is.

I wasn't surprised that my comments became big news in Dallas the next day. I was prepared for that. But I wasn't prepared for the spin some people put on their stories. The fact that Boller is white and Blake is black somehow meant that I was being a racist. I was floored by that. I didn't say anything about black coaches, white coaches, or green coaches. The word I used was *qualified*. Coming from my mouth, though, I guess *qualified* means *black*.

I've heard these accusations before, throughout my career, and I've never understood them. The people I've played with—both here and in San Francisco—know who I am. They know I've helped other players, black and white. If you're a good player and you're working hard, I'll do whatever I can to make your life easier. That's what it means to be part of a team. If I say we need to hire some new, qualified coaches, and someone wants to interpret that as racism, then that's their problem, not mine. If people want to perceive me as a bad guy, then that's what they're going to do. The people who know who I am, they know what I'm about. I'm about honesty.

I'm also the kind of guy who believes in *talking* about things. I'm aware that racism exists in this country. I know it's still a big problem. Part of the reason it's such a problem is that people are afraid to discuss race as an issue. Instead, we just sit there quietly, staying in our own little cliques, hating each other more and more. What we need to do is try to *understand* each other. There are differences between white folks and black folks. You bet your ass there are. Why pretend we're all the same? Instead, let's look at our differences and try to appreciate and understand them. That's what used to piss me off about Harry Edwards in San Francisco: He wanted the black guys to be quiet, to not rock the boat. Well . . . rocking the boat is good. It wakes people up, makes them think.

To a certain degree, being a black man—especially a black man who grew up in the South—defines me. I spend a lot of time in Virginia, and when I'm there, I know what to expect. It's still the old ways there. Blacks are looked down on. If I get stopped by a cop in Virginia, for any reason, I'm going to get harassed. Doesn't matter whether it's a black cop or a white cop. I have to be prepared to say, "Yes sir . . . no sir," and stay on the guy's good side. A couple years ago my brother George was driving one of my cars in Amherst, Virginia, about thirty miles from Gladys. It was a customized Chevy Tahoe with tinted windows. Cars were blowing by him—seventy-five, eighty miles an hour—while he was driving fifty-five. But he was the one who got pulled over.

When the trooper saw that George had a Florida license, then he really became suspicious: a black guy with a Florida license driving a truck with tinted windows and Texas tags. That was all the evidence they needed. They brought out the dogs, ripped the car apart looking for drugs, made him sit there for hours. They do stuff like that in the South. If they see a black guy driving a nice car—and God forbid he has a white woman in the car with him—they're going to go after him. In the end, they gave George a ticket for "illegal tint" or some shit like that, even though the windows were legal in Texas, where the car was sold. I guess the cops had to do something to justify pulling him over. They couldn't give him a speeding ticket because he wasn't speeding. They should have admitted they made a mistake, apologized, and let him go. But they had to cover their asses.

In Dallas, and in a lot of big cities, it's a little different. I never know exactly how I'm going to be treated, but I can tell you this: I won't be treated like a white person. I'm still a country boy, you know? So when I go shopping I usually wear jeans and an old shirt, maybe even sweats. Well, I'm six-five, 250 pounds, and when I walk through the door, you can practically see the fear on the clerks' faces: *Holy shit! It's a big motherfucking black guy! Hang onto your jewelry!* It's like bells ring, sirens start wailing, and people follow me all around, waiting for me to try to steal something. Then, when they find out who I am, they all want to wait on me. They want an autograph. They're all sweet and nice. How transparent is that? What I usually end up doing is going straight to one of the minority clerks for help, so that I don't have to go through all that crap.

If you're white, you can't possibly know what I'm talking about. You've never been through it. You probably think I'm imagining things. But I'm not. When someone tells me it's not like that anymore, that it's just my perception of things, I tell them to wake the hell up. If you don't acknowledge the problem, you can't ever solve it.

One of the things I like about being a professional athlete is that the rules are different than they are in the outside world. A football team is like a mini-society, with one big difference: Blacks are not in the minority; whites are in the minority. But that's not the point. The point is this: In the locker room, you don't have to be so concerned about being politically correct. You can bust each other's balls. You can make racial jokes. You can say "nigger" without starting a riot. And when you see a brother trying to kick it with the white guys, you can call him a "wigger." Most people don't care. You can say almost anything while you're in there playing, horsing around. It's like the military. You're going into battle together, and you have to be able to count on that guy next to you— whether he's black or white. If you don't know what causes him pain, what makes him laugh, what makes him cry . . . then you're screwed.

Plus, it's all about bonding. How do you get a guy to talk to you if you don't know what he likes, what he doesn't like? People on the outside don't understand it. Players understand. Of course, there's a great equalizer in professional sports, and that's money. On the outside, whites generally have more money than blacks. In the NFL, everybody's getting paid well. You're dealing with people from different cultures, different backgrounds, but they're all making a pretty good living. Funny how that changes things.

I'm not trying to suggest that life is perfect in the NFL. It isn't. Not even close. Whether it's intentional or not, the lay-out of a typical NFL locker room promotes segregation and isolation. Think about it: The quarterbacks are together—they're all white; the running backs and wide receivers are together—they're all black; the defensive linemen are to-gether—they're all black. The offensive line is usually mixed, so that's cool; but the secondary is usually all black; and the kickers and punters are white. I understand what they're doing, trying to set it up by position so that players can share knowledge and really bond. But you end up with barriers.

When you're making good money and doing something you love, like playing football, it's easy to be at work for eight hours, smiling, saying what you have to say, doing what you have to do to get by. Most of the time you kick it with your friends, the guys you like, and just do your work. Then, at the end of the day, you go home to your family. It's just like the real world: You work side-by-side with people you like and people you don't like. Most guys, black and white, figure it doesn't really matter, as long as you can play together. The bottom line is winning.

For me, though, it goes beyond that. Maybe it's because I'm getting older, but I have trouble keeping quiet in the locker room. I don't like to simply coexist. I like to provoke. The only way we're ever going to have equality—in football or in the real world—is if we're willing to talk. There will always be people who will try to twist every word into a racist statement, but when you're dealing with the issues, you're making progress. Yeah, you might piss people off, and you might hurt someone's feelings, but at least you're stripping away the ignorance. Words don't hurt people. Ignorance is what gets you killed.

I like to play with people sometimes. I'm a practical joker, a cutup, even after all these years, and I'll try to get my way by saying, "What's the matter with you—won't you give a brother a chance?" Then I sit back and watch the reaction. A lot of white people just fold up and start acting guilty. They shuffle their feet, mumble something about being sorry. That's kind of pathetic. But when the person says, "Get out of my face with that bullshit!" . . . then I know we're getting somewhere.

One of the most interesting things about the O. J. Simpson case was watching the effect it had on our team. Everyone was fascinated, glued to the tube. The Cowboys installed two extra televisions sets in the training room so we could all follow it. As you might expect, we were divided along racial lines. Most of the white guys on the team thought he was guilty, most of the black guys thought he was innocent. But at least we got to a point where we could talk about the issue, and everyone could air their feelings, and then we'd move on. You didn't have to sit there thinking, *O.J. fucking did it, man; he killed them!*—but be afraid to say anything out loud. You could say whatever the hell you wanted. We probably spent twenty minutes every day talking about it, discussing the case. It's strange the way something like that can bring a team together.

At the same time, it pointed out how far apart we are as a society. A lot of people suggested that when O.J. was acquitted, the minority members of the jury were trying to send a message. They were trying to get even for all the bigotry and racism they'd experienced in their lives. I think that's bullshit. Those are the same people who have to rule on black criminals every fucking day. If they thought O.J. was guilty, they would have put his ass in jail. Personally, I don't know whether O.J. is innocent or guilty. I don't think we'll ever know. But I followed the case closely, and I read three books on the subject: Robert Shapiro's, Alan Dershowitz's, and Christopher Darden's. The first two were interesting, because they took you behind the scenes, gave you extra information. I didn't like Darden's book at all, because he didn't really share any facts. He just whined a lot. The fact is, he screwed up at the trial. He didn't do his job. And the police didn't do their job. From everything I saw and heard, I believe at least some of the evidence was planted. To me, that's enough. Don't even look at the rest of the case. I think the jury felt the same way.

The amazing thing about O.J. is that a jury found him not

guilty, but most of America still thought he was guilty. There was no way he could win. One way or another, O.J. was going to pay. That's what happened in the civil trial, when they found him guilty of wrongful death. My problem is, when a man is found guilty or innocent by a jury of his peers, that should be it. Over. End of story. I can understand the pain of the Goldman family and the Brown family. I'm a father, too. But a jury found him innocent. You shouldn't be able to try the man over and over.

What really made me sad was all the hate surrounding that trial, and the way it was reflected in the media. My God, whenever something happened, the media would jump on it. They'd have a black guy speaking for the defense and a white guy speaking for the prosecution. It was never two white people talking about the case, or two black people talking about the case. It was always black and white. They were deliberately fanning the fire. It was sickening.

You know what, though? Fire can be good, too. It's scary; it can burn; but it can also illuminate. We need to understand that racism and bigotry are still among the worst problems facing our society. And we need to understand that education is the key to solving these problems.

But we don't need to waste everyone's time by pulling the race card when it's inappropriate. Let me give you a couple examples. Troy Aikman and I have gotten closer the last two years. I've watched him grow as a person and as a quarterback. And I've watched him suffer. There were a few reporters in Dallas who wrote some nasty shit about Troy in 1996. Among other things, they tried to ruin Troy by suggesting he was a racist because he didn't treat the black guys on the team with enough respect. Well, here's the bottom line: When you're the quarterback, you do what you have to do. Sometimes Troy is out there and he's the only white guy on the field. He starts yelling at his teammates, trying to get them to play better. Does that mean he's a racist? Sometimes I yell when I'm on the field. Does it mean I'm not a racist just because most of the players are black? You see how fucked up it is?

Yelling on the field is not a problem. Football is an emotional game. It's not about racism; it's about taking control. Someone has to be in charge out there. If Troy yells at a few brothers, gets them to play harder, and that makes him a racist . . . then I say, "Go on, Troy! Keep on being a fucking racist. Because you're the quarterback, and I want to know that you're in charge."

That's one thing that bothers me about Troy: He lets people get under his skin. Troy changed a little in '96, man. He was careful. I could tell he was worried about yelling at the guys on offense. He didn't want anyone to think he was mad, so he wouldn't get in their face like he used to. And that ain't Troy. That's not the way he plays. I know he has to be careful about his image, and I know he makes a ton of money from endorsements and shit. But you have to be yourself. You have to be true—especially when you're not doing anything wrong.

The Pro Bowl incident is another example of someone using the race card when it wasn't appropriate. Since the issue has been raised, though, I'll address it. The NFL should make more of an effort to hire qualified minority coaches. But the key word, still, is . . . *qualified*. I think coaches should be chosen, first and foremost, on the basis of ability. I also think that you can't ignore the fact that the great majority of the players in the league are black, and almost all the coaches are white. There are fundamental differences between black players and white players, just as there are differences between men and women, Americans and Europeans. We come from different backgrounds; we've had different experiences. It's great that we have a chance to share those experiences and try to break down the walls that divide us. But there are times when a white player needs to talk to a white coach and a black player needs to talk to a black coach, simply because they're more likely to *understand*. I was sent to a psychologist once, and when I walked into his office, and found out he was white, I politely excused myself. "I think, right now, I'd rather talk to a black doctor," I said.

"Look, Mr. Haley," he said. "I don't have to live in your world to be sympathetic to your situation."

"I know that. But it helps."

It's about finding a comfort zone. Sometimes you need it, sometimes you don't. But it should always be available. Right now it's not. I'll tell you something else: Having a good racial mix on your coaching staff helps with discipline. I've seen a lot of black players try to pull shit on white coaches—and get away with it. Like I said, I've done it myself. There are times when a white coach will let a black player skate just because he feels guilty. In that same situation, a black coach might say, "Fuck you! Get back to work!"

There are a lot of good young black coaches out there who aren't getting an opportunity. And the reason is, there aren't enough black *head* coaches. It's no different than any other profession: If you get a job—if you become the boss—you're going to surround yourself with people who make you comfortable, people you already know; you don't want to have to worry about trusting your assistants. Being different, being *black,* can be the worst thing, because people like being able to say what they want to say. If you're different, if you're an outsider, then everyone has to be careful. So . . . the same people get circulated over and over. Head coaches move from team to team, offensive coordinators get promoted—and they all bring in their buddies. Everyone has a few tokens, to pacify the players, but that's about it. There has to be more of an *effort!*

It's like in California. In order to keep getting state grants, schools have to enroll a certain percentage of minorities. Some people think that's wrong. I think it's necessary, because progress begins with education. White kids generally go to better schools than black kids. Therefore, when they take tests, they get better grades. If they get better grades, they go to better colleges. If they go to better colleges, they get better jobs. And so on. If you're a black kid in the projects, your books are at least two years older than the books the suburban kids are using. Something has to be done to help these kids compete or nothing will ever change.

How do qualified blacks get in the mainstream if there isn't *something* to make a company feel obligated to give a minority a chance? I am *not* talking about just putting a black guy in there, regardless of his abilities. I have no respect for anyone who can't do the job. But if you have a black coach who's knowledgeable, who's ambitious—who deserves a chance—then yeah, I want him in there. And I think the NFL should be making more of an effort to find these people.

See . . . I have this fear. I think one day this big melting pot of ours is going to turn into a huge pile of muck. You won't even be able to tell who the minorities are. Then what are you going to do? Are you going to say, "OK, if you're over six-foot-five, we'll hate you. If you're under four-foot-ten, we'll hate you. If you're fat . . . we'll hate you"? We need people to discriminate against. We need a reason to hate.

This country is getting to be more and more diverse, but that doesn't make the people with power want to relinquish it. I hear these people talking about "the good old days," and it confuses me. It makes me angry. I mean . . . what were the good old days? And who were they good for?

Charles in Charge, Part IX
HOMOPHOBIA

When it comes to homosexuality, the NFL is in the dark ages. The fact is, there have always been gays in professional football, and there always will be gays in professional football. But they stay in the closet. And I don't blame them. It would be very hard for an NFL player to be openly gay. First of all, a lot of players are still scared to death of AIDS. I realize you're not likely to contract the disease during a game, but the fact is, football is a brutal sport. I've come off the field with blood on my jersey, my hands, my face. Sometimes the blood is mine; sometimes it isn't. Am I at risk if I'm playing against someone with AIDS? Probably not. But I can't be certain, and neither can anyone else. There are a lot of myths associated with this disease; there's a lot of ignorance.

Still, that's only part of it. The NFL is a weird, macho world. Every day forty-five or fifty big guys strut around the locker room, buck-naked. A lot of people are insecure about themselves, about their sexuality. You spend five minutes in an any NFL locker room and someone's going to call you a "punk" or a "faggot." It's meant as a joke, but there's no question that it says something about players' attitudes. Gays would not be welcome in the locker room. They'd be ridiculed. They'd be uncomfortable. And they'd make everyone else feel uncomfortable. That's why there's never been an openly gay player in the NFL. If a team suspected a player was gay, in all likelihood they'd get rid of that player. They'd cut him or trade him—anything to avoid having to deal with the problem. Unless he's a star, of course. Then they'd just cover it up.

Personally, I think it's ridiculous. I mean, don't get me wrong. When I was a kid, I didn't even like sleeping with my brothers, so I sure as hell don't want no hairy-ass man in bed with me now. But as far as being my teammate? No problem. What someone does in his bedroom doesn't have any effect on me. As long as he can go out and play football, that's all that matters.

I started thinking about this in 1996, when Troy Aikman's sexual preference was discussed in Skip Bayless's book *Hell Bent,* an "exposé" about the Cowboys. That was big news for a while, because Troy's about the most eligible bachelor in the state of Texas. When I first heard about it, I thought it was hilarious. I ragged Troy for a couple days, you know? He's a good-looking guy, rich, can have any woman he wants. But he's very careful, very private. He doesn't like people knowing his business. Troy has repeatedly denied the rumors about being gay. In fact, whenever the subject comes up, he gets absolutely furious. But that doesn't stop the gossip. I think a lot of people want to hurt Troy, so they invent shit. If you're a football player—especially in Dallas—you don't want people thinking you're gay; it could make your life miserable. It could ruin you.

Here's what I know for certain about Troy Aikman: He's a good man and a hell of a football player. And that's enough. I don't know what goes on behind closed doors, and I don't want to know. I just want to be his teammate.

The truth is, I'd like to think that I'm open-minded about these things. In my heart, though, I know that if I discovered that one of my friends—whether he was a football player or not—was gay, it would change the way I feel about him. At least a little. I don't know how I would react. I'd have to do a lot of soul-searching. Everything I've ever read about anyone who's revealed his homosexuality to his parents or his brothers or sisters, or to his friends . . . it takes a while for them to accept it. I'm sure I'd go through the same kind of process. Homosexuality is not something that I want to advocate to my children, but I have no right to deny people their lifestyle. And I sure as hell don't have a right to deny anyone an opportunity to make a living in their chosen field—even if that field is professional football.

CHAPTER 13

Boys' Night Out

When I moved to California after being drafted by the 49ers in 1986, I was thrown into a completely new world. I was twenty-two at the time, and I should have felt like a big ol' kid in a candy store. Women were everywhere—beautiful women —and they were literally throwing themselves at me. They were coming out of the woodwork, man. That's the way it is when you're a professional athlete. If you've got a little money, if you're famous, the women want a piece of you.

A lot of the rookies acted like they had died and gone to heaven. But I found it scary. I was not coming from a place where you're exposed to that kind of shit all the time. Some of the players who had attended bigger schools were used to being treated like stars. Groupies were nothing new to them;

there were just more of them now. There were countless opportunities, but I found it very hard to close my eyes with
somebody I didn't know. I wanted somebody I cared about—
somebody I trusted—to be there with me. I was lonely. I
missed my mom . . . I missed Karen. To combat the loneliness,
I'd go out with the other guys, and almost immediately we'd
be surrounded by women. These were not shy ladies, let me
tell you. There were no games to be played, no waiting five or
six dates before anything sexual happened. It was like, "Hi!
My place or yours?"

I don't know, maybe I was crazy, but it just wasn't something I was interested in. My response was to ask Karen to
come out and live with me. And then we got married. It was
an eye-opener for her, too. I'd walk out of the locker room
after a game, looking for Karen, and all these women would
be standing around, trying to pick up players. They were aggressive, loud, and gorgeous. Some of them would start talking to me, bumping up against me, flirting, and I'd try to get
away. I'd say, "Hey, please leave me alone. My wife is right
over there." Then we'd get in the car and Karen would say,
"You don't have to be so rude, you know. You can talk to
them."

So, the next time, just to teach her a lesson, I sat there
and talked to the women outside the locker room for about
fifteen minutes. Really charmed them. And, of course, Karen
wouldn't speak to me the whole ride home.

"Look," I said. "You can't have your cake and eat it, too.
You want to be my wife? Then let me hold you right here so

they can see that you're special to me. Otherwise, they're coming after me. These are groupies, and they don't care whether you're married or single. They do not care."

I believe that most men are tempted to commit adultery. They think about it, fantasize about it, all the time. It doesn't matter whether you're a Dallas Cowboy or not. The difference is, when you're a professional athlete, the women are available. There's easy access. They know you're married. You know you're married. But they don't have a problem with it. I've been married for ten years, and I have to say that being married and being a professional athlete is the hardest trial I've ever known. The only way to stay totally faithful is to concentrate on two things: work and family. Go to practice . . . then go home. But you know what? It makes for a boring-ass life, no matter how much you love your wife and kids. I like to kick it with my friends. I like to go to the Cowboys Sports Cafe and shoot some pool. I can't stay trapped behind closed doors for the rest of my life. I'd go crazy.

Celebrity is a double-edged sword. You have money, power, fame—but everyone wants a piece of you. I try to not make judgments; I believe in personal accountability. If you want to mess around with groupies, then at least understand the risks. A lot of younger players have no idea what they're getting into. They think that just because they're young and single, they can do anything they want to do. But it doesn't work like that. There's a price to pay.

Sure, there are some women who are fairly harmless; they just want to do a little star-fucking. But a lot of groupies want more than that. They're looking for husbands, or at least someone to take care of them. They're looking for *money*. Sex they can get anywhere. But when that rent is due, it's nice to have someone they can call for help; someone who will give them nice things every so often.

I also think a lot of groupies are trying to get pregnant, because without getting pregnant they're only in your pocket for one day, or one night, or whatever. If they get pregnant, though, they're in your pocket for *eighteen years!* And what happens—this is the really sleazy thing—is that a lot of women *say* they're pregnant. Then they try to hit the player up for ten or fifteen grand. Then they disappear. That happens all the time. Guys sit in the jacuzzi, hang around the training room, talking about this kind of shit every day. You'll see some sucker walking in, head down, long face, going, "Damn! She says she's pregnant. But I don't think it's mine. Hell, I'm not even sure she's really pregnant."

That usually starts a debate, guys divided on whether the poor bastard should fight it, demand a blood test, or just write a check and hope it all goes away. It's an ugly situation, but you have to ask yourself: *What's it worth?* Are you willing to destroy your life? Your marriage? Just to prove a point? The easiest solution is to give the woman the money. If she's lying, well, call it a learning experience. If she's not lying, then just hope she uses the money to have an abortion. That sounds terrible, I know, but I'd rather not have a kid in this world who

I'd never love; a kid born to a woman who set me up just so she could get pregnant; a kid who came from greed. If it were me—and God knows I hope it never is—I'd pay the money and try to put it behind me.

But some guys are hardheaded. They'll say, "Fuck you! It ain't mine!" And then the girl gets mad, and it turns out she's pregnant, and she has a blood test, and . . . guess what? The guy really is the father. Groupies are smart, though. They know most players won't call their bluff—especially the married guys. Married guys are the best, because they get scared and pay off quicker.

Athletes are no different than anyone else with fame or money. They don't know who they can trust. That's why some men turn to prostitutes. You don't have to worry about being set up. It's just business: cash in exchange for sex. With athletes, the attraction to prostitutes is also related to pressure. Football players feel like they always have to perform; they're always onstage, even when they're not playing. When they get in bed with a prostitute, they can stop performing. She's getting paid to do what she does; he gets to have fun. No expectations, no rules. If he wants to have sex for an hour and be a stud, fine. If he wants to be out in five minutes, that's cool, too. It's his thing.

For a young, single football player the question is this: *Where do I go to meet a good person?* If he meets a woman in a bar, he has no idea if she's sincere or just trying to take his money. Most of them just give up after a while. They hang out in titty bars and try to pick up dancers. They watch a few shows, pick out the girl they like best, and try to pick her up afterward. That way they see everything they're getting; of course, they aren't seeing what they might get later. There are other risks involved. But most of them think the risk is worth taking. These guys are not interested in relationships. Finding a relationship takes too much work. Funny thing is, most of them eventually do build some kind of relationship with the dancers. The sexual thing goes away, but they keep coming back to the club, just to talk. Sometimes you'll see a dancer with a guy and they're no more than friends. The sexual part is over, but they still like to kick it. It's kind of cute, in a way.

Personally, I only go to places like that two or three times a year. I don't like being teased. I think that sometimes things have to be left to the imagination. You have to fool yourself into believing that you're not lusting. Know what I'm saying? You see a woman in a bar and she's fully dressed and you're going, "Damn, she's fine!" That's one thing. But there are lines you can't cross. You go into a titty bar with your tongue hanging out and you start drinking . . . Trouble, man. Big fucking trouble. You're setting yourself up for failure. I don't need that. I want to be in control of my life.

———————

There's a misconception about the Dallas Cowboys: that the franchise is out of control, the inmates are running the asylum, and Barry Switzer is responsible. But I have to tell you, the incidents that were so widely publicized in Dallas in 1996

—stories about drug use and infidelity and wild partying—
could just as easily have happened in any other NFL city. And
they sure as shit happened in Dallas long before Barry was the
coach. Guys were doing all kinds of crazy stuff under Jimmy
Johnson, too. They always have, always will.

When I first arrived in Dallas in '92 I went out to a private
party. Man, I was stunned. I saw all kinds of bizarre behavior.
There were beautiful women all over the place, with dresses
hiked up to their butt. There was drug use. And there were a
whole bunch of young players there, just acting wild. I looked
around and realized there was no talking to these guys. They
were out for a good time. And I thought, *Damn! I can't get
caught up in this shit now. I just got traded.*

I stayed for about ten minutes and then called a cab and
went back to my hotel. I didn't care if my quick exit pissed
anyone off. I'm not a trusting soul, and I wasn't about to trust
my whole career—*my life*—to a bunch of people I didn't even
know, and end up with my ass in jail.

Too many athletes get the money and the fame and all of a
sudden forget who they are. They want to get bigger and bigger. They want to please everybody, run the whole show. So
they do a top-notch and go way out there. That's how they get
in big trouble. They should step back and say, "Okay, I've
made it. I've got a little money. Now . . . what really makes
me happy?" Instead, they go crazy—throwing money all over
the place, using drugs, drinking too much, having sex with
three or four girls at a time. I mean, what the fuck can one guy

do with four women? I guess you can live out your fantasies, but I'll tell you, I've got a wife at home and I catch hell just trying to please her. What would I do with *four* women?

———————

As a rule, I believe that people are responsible for their own actions. Football players are grown men, even if they don't always act that way. So I try not to be nosy. But if I hear that something's going on, especially with a friend, I'll get involved. I'll tell them to slow down, try to relax a little. If they want to talk to me, I'll listen. I'd want my friends to do me the same way. If they see me out of control, then I want them to slap my head. Don't let me fall down and get run over by the truck before you tell me the truck is coming.

Unfortunately, you don't always see the truck. I didn't see it with Michael Irvin.

Michael went through hell in '96. In March he and a former Cowboy, Alfredo Roberts, were discovered by police in a Dallas hotel room, along with two young women. The cops also found some cocaine and marijuana, and drug and sexual paraphernalia. The case went to trial, but Mike eventually pleaded no contest to a felony charge of cocaine possession and was placed on probation and ordered to fulfill a community service obligation. He also received a five-game suspension from the NFL.

Now, I like to think of myself as a good friend of Michael's. We hang out at the Cafe together, we shoot pool, have a few beers. But after that, I go home. Mike likes to stay out. He likes being the center of activity. He's very charismatic. He talks a lot, he dresses great, and he commands attention. So even though we're friends, we have different lives. If he was heading for some kind of a crash, I missed it. People have asked me, "What do you tell Michael when you see him having trouble?" Well, the point is, I didn't see him having trouble. And by the time somebody gets caught, it's too late.

Thomas "Hollywood" Henderson came out and blasted the Cowboys after Michael's arrest. He talked about how Michael obviously had a terrible drug problem. Well, how hard is it to kick somebody in the nuts when he's down? The media was already running through Mike's butt—I saw one magazine with a picture of Mike on the cover with a great big white smear under his nose, like the man doesn't do anything but snort coke—and here comes an ex-football player, a *Cowboy*, for Christ's sake, who's been through all the drug stuff himself, and he's going to jump on the bandwagon? That pissed me off.

People should remember that Michael Irvin has never failed a drug test. *Never!* So maybe he deserves the benefit of the doubt. I know I didn't try to lecture him on right or wrong. Mike knows the difference between right and wrong. He has sixteen brothers and sisters. When he was a kid he didn't have much, but he gives to everyone now. He gives with every ounce of himself: time, money, energy. His parents did a great job. He's one of the nicest people I've ever known. So when he was going through all this, I just tried to be his friend. I talked to his wife and said, "Please, stand by your man." I hung out with him and shot pool, tried to lift his spirits.

The one thing I regret is that I didn't come out and say something publicly to try to help Mike. There were only a few people on the team—Troy Aikman, Daryl Johnston, Emmitt Smith—who could have gone into the courtroom during the trial to stand by Mike without risking character assassination. If I had come out and supported Mike publicly, the media would have interpreted it as me condoning what he did. That's why a lot of players didn't say anything. They were scared. I think Mike understood, though. I think he realized what we were trying to tell him, which was, *We're behind you, man. If you've got a problem or something, fine. Get it taken care of. But we still love you.*

That incident hurt Michael bad. And not just Mike, but his whole family. His wife, his kids, his brothers and sisters, his mom. They had to listen to all the sordid details every day. Mike felt horrible about that. It ate him up. I think he's on his way back now, but it's going to take some time. We're down in the Bible Belt here—there's a church every few miles—but Dallas is a city that does not forgive easily.

Everyone makes mistakes in their lives. So before you throw that first stone, take a good hard look at yourself. Look at the things you do every day. You might not use drugs, but maybe you're messing around on your wife. Or maybe you drink too much. Everybody does something that they know is wrong. What's important is whether you learn from your mistakes, whether you try to be a good person. Michael wasn't even given a chance to say, *"Hey, I screwed up. I messed up royally. I FUCKED UP! All I want you to do now is give me an opportunity to make it right."*

He deserved at least that much.

Instead, Mike was harassed all season: by fans, by the media, by the police. People even starting inventing shit. In January a woman named Nina Shahravan accused two men, including Cowboys tackle Erik Williams, of raping her while a third man held a gun to her head. The incident allegedly occurred at Erik's house. And the man with the gun, she claimed, was Michael Irvin. She also said Michael videotaped the incident. To me, this was obviously a setup. The woman was out for money, and she probably figured she had two easy marks. How hard would it be to convince people that Michael was a rapist? Or Big E, who had been accused of sexual assault by a seventeen-year-old topless dancer in '95? Everyone hated those guys so much that people were willing to believe any accusation. This woman made outrageous claims, and instead of checking it out first, the cops just made a public announcement. And all of a sudden Michael was back on the cover of national magazines . . . on the evening news . . . on *Nightline* for Christ's sake.

The cops didn't even bother to ask him, "Where were you?" Isn't that the first thing you should do when you're investigating someone? Find out if it was even possible for him to commit the crime? On the night that he was supposedly at Erik Williams's house, assaulting this woman, Michael was at the Cowboys Sports Cafe. He had thirty witnesses saying he was there. But everyone wanted to believe he was guilty. Everyone wanted to assume the worst.

Same with Big E. He never denied the woman was in his house, or that he had used a video camera. The way I understand it, Big E said he started taping himself after what happened in '95, strictly for protection. I guess he figures if there's a video camera rolling when you're having sex, no one's going to accuse you of rape. It's crazy, I know, but that's what it's come to. Usually when somebody tapes a sexual encounter, it's just for kicks, to show off in front of their friends later. Personally I can't imagine doing that, because I don't think that what goes on in someone's bedroom should be seen again. Especially when it's someone like Big E, who weighs about 325 pounds. I used to kid him and say, "Man, I see your fat ass at work every day. Why the hell would I ever want to see you making love to a woman?"

But that's how bad it's gotten. You have to take outrageous precautions when you're a professional athlete. Even when you're smart enough to stay out of trouble, there's always the possibility that someone will try to ruin your career—just for the sheer hell of it. And believe me, these accusations do irreparable harm. After an eleven-day investigation, the Dallas police announced that the woman had recanted her story. No charges were ever filed. But the damage was done. I saw Michael one day in the locker room and he was just sitting there, looking like a beaten man, shaking his head, going,

"Damn, they're really out to get me, huh? They'll even make shit up."

Michael is a hell of a great guy, regardless of what's happened to him. I love him. He's gentlemanly, friendly, trusting. Unfortunately, society is now going to fail him, because he'll stop trusting. He'll stop seeing the good in people and start looking for the bad. Michael used to be the kid of guy who, as soon as he met you, he'd take you in as family. But now he's not so open with people.

Maybe that's the way it has to be if you're a Dallas Cowboy. When you're bigger than life, you have to be careful. Some people are always going to be out to get you. And when you fuck up, they'll tear you apart. They'll show no mercy.

Not many people can stand living in the spotlight. The scrutiny you face as a Cowboy is unbelievably intense. I sincerely believe that if other teams were subjected to this kind of media coverage, you'd hear the same kinds of stories. But I've never seen anyone go after players the way they went after Michael in '96. It was almost as if everyone—the media, the cops, even the fans—wanted to see him put in jail. He was paying the price of celebrity.

He was paying for being a Dallas Cowboy.

As bad as I felt about what happened to Michael, I felt even worse about Leon Lett. Leon is one of the best defensive tackles in the NFL. And he's a good kid. I've always thought of him as a son, or at least a younger brother. I tried to help him grow. I did him the way Ronnie Lott did me. In the meeting room once, we could see on film that Leon wasn't playing up to his level, and I got very angry with him. I ripped into him in front of everyone. Man, was that sucker mad. He went out to practice that day and he hurt people. He busted up the whole offensive line. Afterward, I went up to him and said, "You want to whip my ass, Leon?" He just said, "Get the fuck out of my face, man!" and walked away. But I wouldn't let it go. I was determined to be his friend. I saw something in him that reminded me of myself. I cared for him. Pretty soon we got to be close friends.

It kills me to see what's happening to Leon—to watch him throw his career away. He was suspended for violating the league's substance abuse policy in 1995, but came back strong in '96. In fact, he was having a great season, an All-Pro season; hell, he might have been named Defensive Player of the Year. In December, though, Leon's world came crashing down. The NFL said he had violated the substance abuse policy again, and this time he was going to be suspended for a year.

A year!

When I heard that, I cried. It was one of the saddest days of my life. I talked to Leon for a couple hours that night, tried to encourage him, tell him to hang in there, but he was devastated. Truth is, so was I. Leon had it all, man. He took the little bit of knowledge I gave him and he went out there and perfected it. I watched him grow, to the point where he was at the top of his game. I wanted him to take other guys under his wing and do them like I did him—like Ronnie did me. I believe in that. Every great player should pass his knowledge on. Now the chain was broken, and that made me mad.

Plus, I cared about Leon as a friend. He's really a very sensitive, thoughtful young man, and I was concerned about how he would handle this. The first time he got suspended people would whisper in the dark a little. But now it was like, *Damn! He got suspended for a year. He must really have a problem.*

Leon's name will always be associated with drugs now. Commentators will get on TV and the first thing out of their mouths will be, "Leon Lett, coming off a year's suspension for violating the league's drug policy." Or when someone's writing an article, somewhere in that story—whether it's good, bad, or indifferent—will be a reference to drug use. They'll bring up his history. As soon as I heard about his suspension, I could see all that. I knew what he was in for, and it tore my heart out.

There's a part of me that's angry with Leon. The day before the suspension came down he told me, "They're messing with me, man. They're trying to fuck me over." I said, "What are you talking about? That's bullshit! As soon as my back gets better I'm gonna whip your ass!"

I doubt if I could really do it—Leon's a strong, violent motherfucker—but I'll try anyway. I'll knock a little sense into him. A man has to keep his mind on his money and his money on his mind. He cannot afford to give back three or four million dollars. That's outrageous. It's *stupid!* Some guys say, "Well, it's my money." But it's not just your money. And it's not just you. I think of it like this: As a professional athlete, I can bring up the standard of living for my whole family—for generations. My kids . . . my brother's kids . . . my grandchildren. They might not have to endure the pain I went through. That's the way I look at it, and that's what I try to instill in these dumb fuckers. But most of them don't see it. They don't give a damn. They don't look at the big picture.

The bottom line is, when you're done playing the game, and you walk into a store and say, "Hey, remember me? I played in the NFL and I'm a hell of a nice guy," they're going to look at you and say, "Well, that's great. Fantastic. That'll be $255 . . . *please!*" It's about the money, and you cannot let people take the money away from you over some stupid shit like drugs. Especially when you've already been caught once with your hand in the cookie jar. After that, stay the hell away from the cookie jar. There's no excuse for getting caught a second time—unless you have a serious problem.

Maybe that's the case with Leon. I don't know. If it is, I'll be there for him. I love him and I want him to realize that I'll be by his side through good and bad. I'll do everything in my power to make sure he doesn't get in trouble again. If I have to go to rehab meetings with him, I'll do it. Whatever it takes. Not because I condone what he did, but because I believe in him and I care about him. You can't stop being somebody's friend just because he did something wrong. When a football player gets in trouble, it's like anybody else—friends have to rally around him. They have to hug him and support him and let him know he's not alone.

I have no easy explanation for what happened with the Cowboys in 1995 and 1996, when seven players were suspended for violating the league's drug policy. I have a theory, though: When you win that many Super Bowls, it does something to you. Your confidence grows. Your chest gets bigger. You kind of leave your body a little bit. When you're walking down the street you bump into people without even knowing it, because they let you do things, they treat you differently. When that happens, players take on different attitudes. They think they can get away with anything. Maybe that's the culprit.

Personally, though, I think that's just an excuse. Bill Walsh always used to tell the rookies, "Gentlemen, the scholarships are over. You're on your own now. If you want to fuck up, it's on your back, not mine." I agree. That's why I don't think it's fair to blame the coach when a player gets caught using drugs. Habits don't start overnight. There were players using drugs on the Dallas Cowboys long before Barry Switzer came to town. And there will be players using drugs long after he's gone.

Drugs aren't the only problem. Just the most publicized. The media focuses on players who get arrested for possession of cocaine or who fail drug tests. Those guys are treated like the scum of the earth. The NFL likes to take a real hard-line stance on drug use, too. It is my personal opinion, however, that alcohol is the biggest problem in professional sports. Even in college sports. I firmly believe the reason we didn't win more games at James Madison was because a lot of players were drinking almost nonstop—every night, every day. That's when everyone learns how to drink, right? In college? I never tasted alcohol until I left home. Then I had my first beer. Then I had my second. It started out as a social thing; before long, it was part of my life.

It's the same way in the NFL. Everywhere you go, alcohol is available. You walk into a restaurant, somebody hands you a beer. You walk into a party, somebody hands you a drink. There's an endless supply. After a while, you fall into a habit. You're drinking all the time. When I was younger I used to call myself a functional alcoholic. I still go through spells where I drink heavily. Hell, after a game, we'll go out to dinner, maybe six or seven of us, and spend six hundred dollars on alcohol alone. We drink and drink and drink—champagne, wine, beer, hard liquor, you name it. We're celebrating; and when football players celebrate, they drink. There are only a few guys in the league who don't like to drink.

A lot of it has to do with camaraderie. When I was with the 49ers, we'd finish work at 4:30, 5:00, and traffic would be just hellacious. So we'd go across the street to Bennigan's and we'd kill time by eating, drinking, shooting pool. It's the same way with the Cowboys. The Cowboys Cafe is less than a mile from the practice facility; plus, just about everybody lives in the Valley Ranch area, so that makes it convenient. You show up around five or six, stay until eight . . . nine . . . ten . . . whatever. By then the traffic has thinned out and you can cruise on home.

Of course, by then you're too drunk to drive. A lot of guys drive anyway, though. I know I have. But seeing Erik Williams mess up his car a couple years ago really opened my eyes. I don't know whether he was legally drunk or not, but seeing him in there like that gave me a chill. That shit is bad news. Now, if I know I'm going to be drinking, I usually take a limo. And at the end of the night I'm often the one trying to take the car keys away from other players, or telling them to stop drinking if they're getting out of control. We may have to tussle a little bit, but I always win. I'm not going to let anybody get a ticket or get killed. I'll look out for them.

Our whole society has a problem with alcohol, but I think it's worse among athletes in general and football players in particular. Maybe it's a way to deal with the pressure . . . or the pain. I don't know. But I do know it's a problem.

You used to see a lot more cocaine and marijuana use, but since the NFL instituted tougher drug testing policies, most players have switched back to alcohol. If the league was really interested in working with players who have substance abuse problems, it would focus on alcohol—the legal drug. It's hard to prove someone has a drinking problem, though, because drug tests can't deal effectively with it. That's one of the main reasons alcohol has become so popular again. Cocaine and marijuana show up days, even weeks later. Not alcohol. You can go out and drink all night, and the next morning your system is clean. And players are doing precisely that, especially the younger players. I see it a lot. Guys drink all week, and then go out the night before a game, too, as if they have something to prove. I'm not talking about casual drinking. I'm talking about getting hammered. It's as if they think they can do anything and get away with it. The older guys are different. We've tried all that shit, and we know the body can't handle it. Not for long, anyway.

The NFL has to realize that times have changed. People haven't stopped their habits; they've *altered* their habits. The league also has to treat everyone equally. I think what happened with Brett Favre in 1996 was complete bullshit. Brett told the league that he was addicted to painkillers. As part of his treatment program he was subjected to a league-imposed ban on alcohol. Well, Brett didn't think that was fair, since he'd come forward on his own and made it quite clear that he had a specific problem: painkillers. So he fought it. By the end of the season, it was widely reported that the league backed off and lifted the ban on alcohol.

I don't blame Brett for challenging the NFL. If he felt he was being treated badly, then he should have fought it. My problem is this: We've always been told that once you're in the program, you're in. There are guys who get stopped for driving under the influence and never test positive for anything, never get arrested. But they wind up in the league's drug and alcohol program, getting tested for everything under the sun. When they try to appeal, they get shot right down. But with Brett Favre, because he's the golden boy, the league handles the situation differently. Is that right? And what about the media? Why didn't they climb up Brett's asshole the way they did with Michael?

It's not like there isn't some history there. Brett has a reputation as a drinker. But nobody really cares, because he's the franchise. He's the MVP. He's a white superstar in a predominantly black league. Better to cover it up and get him back on the field. That's the way it works: The NFL covers up stuff on some people, and on others they make it public.

I have nothing against Brett Favre personally. I think he's a great athlete and a hell of a quarterback. But if the NFL reduces his punishment to the point where he only has to be tested for painkillers, that's wrong. He'd be allowed to drink. Why doesn't anyone get upset about that? Why doesn't anyone holler fire? If I ever went to a drug rehab program, by the time the media got through with the story I'd be hooked on crack, acid, heroin . . . everything. Because I ain't no golden boy.

I'll tell you . . . if I had been in the league's substance abuse program, and Brett Favre got off easy? I'd have sued those suckers, man, because it's wrong. They're showing favoritism, and that's why they have no credibility.

Charles in Charge, Part X
IDOL CHATTER (MICHAEL AND MICHAEL)

One of the highlights of my career did not even occur on the football field. It happened on an army base in San Antonio, Texas, in February 1996. I was in town to see the NBA All-Star Game. Afterward, I went to a private party with William Fuller, a friend of mine who played for the Philadelphia Eagles. We were hanging out, shooting pool, when all of a sudden a buzz swept through the room. Heads starting turning, people started yelling. I looked toward the door . . . and there he was . . .

Michael Jordan!

Now, you might think it's strange for one professional athlete to be in awe of another, but it happens, man. It happens a lot. Michael was bigger than big. He was an icon. I'd been a fan of his for years, and now I had a chance to meet him. I was truly excited, but I wanted to play it cool. There were a few other NBA All-Stars in the room—Penny Hardaway, Shaquille O'Neal—and they were hollering at Michael, too, trying to get his attention. *Everybody* wanted a piece of the guy. But he just made a beeline for the pool table. I started looking around, trying to figure out who he had spotted. He kept walking in my direction . . . staring . . . smiling. All of a sudden he was standing right next to me, acknowledging me, telling me how much he liked the way I played football. I was shocked.

Imagine that: *Michael Jordan admired me!*

After a few minutes we settled into a game of pool— Michael and his partner (sorry, I don't remember who it was) against me and William. Michael likes to talk a lot of trash whenever he's competing, even if it's just a friendly rack of pool. It didn't work this time, though. We still won.

Not that I really cared. I just appreciated being there, sharing a table with Michael Jordan. I felt like a little kid. I'll tell you something, though—seeing him in that situation, up close, made me realize what life must be like for him. He can't leave his house without being mobbed by people. He has to have a bodyguard with him almost all the time. I can't imagine that. I mean, I envy the fact that he's a phenomenal athlete and he's super rich, but he has absolutely no private life. I don't know how he handles it. Somehow, though, he does. Michael is incredibly poised. He's a hell of a player and a great person. For a little while that night he made me feel like an equal, which was really nice. I could talk to him. I didn't have to stand there with my mouth shut, afraid to say the wrong thing.

I was a lot less cool the first time I met one of my heroes: Michael Jackson. I'd been a fan of his since I was a little kid, when I used to buy Jackson Five records. It was in honor of Michael that I started wearing a single glove on the football field. I just love the guy and I love his music. I think he's the greatest performer ever.

Well, once, when I was with the 49ers, the team made a trip to London, and while we were there we had an opportunity to attend one of Michael's concerts. We were also invited backstage to meet him. At the time I was really into imitating Michael, singing his songs around the locker room, dancing all over the place. So, naturally, some of the guys were teasing me, saying, "Hey, Charles, you gonna moonwalk for Michael when you meet him?"

I laughed. "Sure," I said. "Whatever he wants."

When I got backstage, though, I was completely tongue-tied. Michael was being very friendly, chatting with us, telling us how he didn't know that much about football, but that his brothers were big fans. And I couldn't say a word. I completely froze.

Still, it was an honor just being in the same room with him. I know a lot of people put Michael down, but whatever you think of him personally, it doesn't diminish his talent. He's a true artist. Everyone copies him—that's the ultimate tribute. Unfortunately, whenever you become the greatest at something, there's a certain segment of society that will try to tear you down. I tend not to listen.

CHAPTER 14

A Season in Hell

August 1996—

If I hadn't rushed back to play in the Super Bowl, things might have been different. If I'd just chilled, maybe I could have squeezed two or three more years out of this old body. Then again, maybe not. Hindsight, man . . . a complete waste of time.

Training camp was supposed to be a piece of cake. Everyone had agreed that there was no reason for me to practice much, and I sure as hell wasn't going to be doing any hitting. The idea was to give my back a rest and hopefully be ready by the start of the regular season. I'd stay in shape by jogging, stretching, lifting weights a little bit. Unfortunately, even that proved to be too much. I was running on the field one day when I felt a slight twinge in my back. I don't know how it happened; I don't know why. But it got worse every day. From that point on, I was always sore.

By the second week in August, I was undergoing pain management again. This time, though, the injections didn't seem to have the same effect, so I knew I was in trouble. On Monday, August 12, I played about half of a preseason game against the New England Patriots. It was the first live action I'd seen since the Super Bowl. Don't ask me why I played; I have no idea. I wasn't supposed to play. Nobody forced me. But people were giving me strange looks, asking me when I'd be ready, and pretty soon I felt like I had to get out there on the field.

I was being hardheaded. I should have just stayed on the sideline. I wanted to help, though, and actually I kind of had fun in that game. It felt good to run around a little, actually make contact after all those months. The adrenaline and the emotion—and the needle, of course—carried me through that game. The next day, though, my back started getting tight again. Two days later I went in for another injection. *Damn!* The season hadn't even started, and already I was back on the treadmill.

We opened up in Chicago, against the Bears. To say we did not play like Super Bowl champions would be an understatement. But then, we weren't exactly the same team we were seven months earlier. Michael Irvin was serving a five-game suspension for violating the NFL's drug policy; Shante Carver, a defensive end, was serving a six-game suspension. Jay Novacek, our starting tight end, was out with a back injury. Half the offensive line was banged up. And I was a mess.

The Bears took advantage of our problems. In fact, they kicked the shit out of us, 22–6. For me, the game took a real physical toll. The Bears came right at me, double-teamed me most of the day. I saw a lot of drive blocks, offensive linemen power-stepping to get into me. I realized pretty quickly that this was how it was going to be all season. Playing in the NFL is like being an animal in the wild: There's no mercy. The wounded are hunted down and killed. It was important for me to fight back in that game, to not seem weak. I had to use my quickness and experience and knowledge to offset their power. I was able to hit guys at weird angles, so that I wouldn't feel the blows as intensely. When they did hurt me, I tried not to let it show, because I knew this game would set the tone for the entire season. If anything worked on me, everyone else would pick up on it. The tape would be out the next morning and offensive linemen all over the league would be plotting their strategy. I was determined not to let that happen.

The next week I had a sack and three tackles in a 27–0 win over the Giants. Not bad. Afterward, though, I was really hurting. I went in for an MRI that week, but the test showed no new damage. I was starting to feel like I was going out of my mind, because I knew there was something seriously wrong, something that had probably happened in the middle of training camp. But I decided to keep playing.

On September 15 we lost to the Indianapolis Colts, 25–24. The media was hammering us relentlessly by that time. After all, we were the defending Super Bowl champs, and we were off to a 1–2 start. I didn't like the losing, but to be honest, I was more concerned with my deteriorating physical condition. At one point against the Colts I got hit really hard and lost the feeling in my left leg. In all my years of playing, with all my back problems, that had never happened before. Pain was one thing, losing sensation was another. It was scary. I went to the sidelines and told the doctor and the trainer that my whole leg had gone numb; even after several minutes, I still had no feeling in my quadriceps. They looked at me, examined me a little bit, and then said they couldn't find any problem, which was ridiculous! I'm not a doctor, but I know bullshit when it's coming my way. I knew that moment—right there while I was on the sideline—that I was going to need back surgery again. I knew it was just a matter of time. The pain was too severe, too unusual.

After the doctor finished examining me, I walked over to Barry Switzer and said, "This is the last game I'm going to play." After the game, I told him again. I was dead serious, and he knew it. He looked at me, and I could tell he understood. Barry's more of a father figure than anything else. He feels for his players.

"It's okay, Charles," he said. "If you're hurting that bad, you shouldn't play. Take the time you need and get well."

Of course, he didn't realize that I wasn't going to get well—not for a long, long time.

"Charles, I recommend you do not play football anymore."

Those were Dr. Watkins's exact words. I'd gone out to California the day after the Indianapolis game, because I wanted to speak with someone I could trust, someone who wouldn't lie to me. The pain in my back and legs was so intense that it frightened me. Not just the pain, but the numbness. I couldn't function normally. It felt like a hernia or a pulled groin or something. I couldn't walk without a pronounced limp. I couldn't even urinate without holding on to the wall for support; and then I'd stand there and pee forever. It was like there was something wrong with my bladder. Everything was messed up, even my bodily functions.

Dr. Watkins ordered a bunch of tests—X rays, another MRI—and then asked me to come into his office. He was very careful, thorough, the way he always is, but his tone was different this time. He pointed to the X ray and said that a small fragment of disk had broken off . . . again! That's what was causing the pain. I expected him to say I needed rest, or maybe even surgery. But I wasn't prepared for such a dramatic recommendation:

" . . . *not play football anymore.*"

He just came right out with it. I didn't say anything at first. I just sat up in my chair. Dr. Watkins is a nice man, and he's usually very upbeat. This time he was much more serious. The words came out of his mouth and I froze. It was like getting hit in the face. I thought, *Hold it right there, baby! Did I hear you right?* I got dizzy. I had to grab the arms of the chair to keep from falling over. If his secretary hadn't been in the room, staring right at me, I think it probably would have brought a tear to my eye.

———————

I called my wife from Dr. Watkins's office, to give her the bad news. She was sad, but supportive, told me to come on home. Then I went straight to the airport and caught the next flight to Dallas. On the plane, I called my mother. She told me she loved me, tried to cheer me up, but I was pretty much inconsolable. Once again I was being told that my career was over; I was being forced out, rather than leaving on my own terms. It happens to every athlete eventually, but I wasn't ready. Not yet.

I needed something to drown my sorrows, so I started drinking on the plane. In fact, I was so depressed that I stayed drunk for the next few days. I didn't want to be around my own family, even though they were the ones who would have given me the most support. I couldn't face my wife and children; I couldn't face my responsibilities. I'm not proud of that, but it's the truth. When I got off the plane I went to the Cowboys Sports Cafe. Leon Lett was there, Godfrey Myles—my boys! They couldn't lift my spirits, though. As a matter of fact, what really hurt was that those guys started getting down, feeling sorry for me. Instead of them making me laugh, I was making them cry. That just made things even worse. So I made a decision that I didn't want to be around them, either. I climbed into a bottle by myself for a little while, lived in a hotel room. I don't remember much about it. I just remember wanting to anesthetize myself. So I kept drinking.

Karen eventually caught up with me. I called home after a couple days and she came and picked me up. She was cool about the whole thing. We've been together ten years, so she knows me pretty well. She knows that I don't handle bad news very well. The way I deal with it is to run away for a few days, sort out my feelings, and then try to attack it. She didn't know where I was, so she was scared, of course, but she didn't lecture me. Not for the first few days, anyway. She backed up, gave me some room, which was exactly what I needed.

By the end of the first week off, I was starting to feel better, which is always the worst thing that can happen, because then you start lying to yourself, convincing yourself that maybe the injury really isn't that bad after all. By the end of the second week I said, "Shit, the doc's wrong. I've played with this before, I can do it again. All I have to do is get the strength back." So I started driving to Valley Ranch and working out. But I went at odd times—late at night, early in the morning. You see, guys don't respect anyone who isn't playing. Doesn't matter what you've accomplished in the past, or how seriously you're hurt. No one wants to hear your troubles. If you can't play, you shouldn't be hanging around the locker room. If you're in there, people start coming up to you, raising an eyebrow, giving you that look: *"Well? When are you coming back? This week? Next week?"* I didn't want to go through that this time. I didn't want to argue with anyone. My temper is too quick. I was really on edge, and I didn't want to say anything I might regret. I'd lost a lot of friends that way, and I wanted to keep the few that I had left. So I took myself away from the team. I'd work out when no one else was around. I'd get on the stepper, lift weights, go in the steam room. I'd lose myself in there for hours.

Meanwhile, on the field, the Cowboys kept struggling. We lost to Buffalo and then barely beat Philadelphia. After five weeks we were 2–3. In Game 6, Michael Irvin returned, and it was like the entire team came to life. He caught five passes and we breezed past Arizona, 17–3. More than anything else that game pointed out just how valuable a player Michael is. There had been a debate in Dallas the past few years: Who's better—Troy, Emmitt, or Michael? Well, I'll tell you, those are the big three, and we had two of them the first five games of the season, but we played like shit. It just seemed like we couldn't win without Michael, so I guess that ends the argument.

Personally, though, I don't believe in excuses. We still had a lot of talent. We just weren't playing with courage. Players were hanging their heads and the coaches had no vision. As a team, we played scared football most of the season. We were afraid to take chances. God, I hate that! You don't win in the NFL if you don't have balls. And we castrated ourselves.

On Monday, October 21, I walked into a team meeting for the first time in four weeks. We were going over our scouting report for that week's opponent: the Miami Dolphins. I hadn't told anyone that I was coming back. That's not the way it works. If you're questionable, and you show up for the scouting report meeting on Monday, it's like carrying a sign that says *"I'm ready to play."* When you walk into that room, you're making a commitment.

I really wasn't in any shape to play. My back was still sore and my conditioning sucked. But this was an opportunity I could not miss. The Dolphins' new coach was Jimmy Johnson, and he and I had a little score to settle.

The anticipation of playing against Jimmy carried me through a week of practice. I was high on emotion. There was so much hype before the game, twice as much media coverage as usual, which is saying a lot when you're talking about the Cowboys. Most of the players—and coaches—were trying to downplay everything. You know, they'd sit around telling reporters how much they still love and respect Jimmy. But man, I'm out with these suckers, you know? I'm in the locker room with them every day. I know what's up. I hear what they're saying. Everybody on the Cowboys wanted to *kick Jimmy's ass!*

That's precisely what happened, too. We went down to Miami and beat the Dolphins, 29–10. It was sweet, man, one of the sweetest victories of my life. I didn't get a single sack, or even a tackle. But I started and played most of the game. I spent a lot of time in their backfield, harassing Dan Marino, a quarterback I respect very much. If you're going to beat the Dolphins, you have to shut down Marino. On this day he completed only twelve of twenty-seven passes.

We had a chance to rub it in at the end. We were on the Miami 7-yard line with two minutes left, but Barry decided to run the clock out. Afterward, everyone was talking about "character" and "respect" and "compassion." Hell with that. I wanted to score as many points as we could. Barry and Jerry and most of the players were in the locker room talking about how it was just another football game, and there was no need to go for the jugular. *Bullshit!* When Jimmy was in Dallas he wanted to take credit for everything, like he was bigger than the whole franchise, and the players were just decorations. Now he knew better. The second that game ended I ran across the field and started screaming at him: "HOW 'BOUT THEM FUCKIN' COWBOYS?!"

He didn't answer me, didn't even make eye contact. He just ran off the field as fast as he could. I know Jimmy used to jog a lot, but he must have become a sprinter in Miami, because he was moving, man. That motherfucker's face was all pink-red, you know? Like his head was gonna explode. I'll tell you, he ran off that field faster than anyone I've ever seen. I couldn't even keep up with him. Watching him run away like that, humiliated, I felt so good that I almost forgot about my back problems.

The euphoria didn't last long, though. We played Philadelphia the next week, and I took a beating. They were double-teaming me from the jump, and I kept getting all twisted around. On one play I was rushing against the tackle. I shook him inside and then went outside, ready to get the sack. But Ricky Watters, the Eagles' running back, was hanging back, pass blocking. He picked me up, came right at me full speed. I saw him coming and tried to spin back inside, but it was too late. My body was going in about three different directions when he hit me. I felt something go right away, a sharp pain in my lower back. It sliced right down my spine and into my legs. Before I even hit the ground, I was thinking . . .

This is bad.

I played a few more downs that day, but each time I went back to the bench, the pain intensified. By halftime I had taken five Vicodin. I'd had an injection that week, too. I think I have a pretty high threshold for pain. I mean, I'll do almost anything to get back on the field. But this kind of pain was beyond anything I had ever experienced. I simply could not deal with it. Nerve pain is like that—it seeps into every corner of your body and mind. It beats you down, makes you want to cry. I sat on the bench most of the second half, listening to players walking by, going, "You gonna play? You ready? What's the problem, Charles?" Shit like that. Nobody cared about me. None of the players, none of the coaches. Not one of them gave a damn about what was going through my head, what my body was feeling like. At that moment in time, the only thing that mattered was that I was dressed in my uniform. I was *there*, so I was expected to endure the pain and get my ass back out on the field and play. Just like always.

We lost to the Eagles, 31–21. Our record was now 5–4. Forget about winning another Super Bowl; we were looking like a team that might have trouble making the playoffs. I really wasn't thinking about any of that, though. Shortly after the game ended one of the defensive line coaches came up to me and said, "Damn, you really took a pounding out there, Charles. If you can handle that, you can probably play the rest of the season." I just looked at him. His reaction confirmed what I'd always suspected: In their eyes I was not a human being; a man. I was strictly a piece of meat. And I wasn't even *prime* beef any more; I was *aged.*

I stayed in Dallas for the next four or five days. By this time everyone was starting to get their act together. The trainer, Jim Maurer; Dr. Vandermeer; Dr. Zamorano—they were all telling me to see Dr. Watkins and let him make the decision. I think everyone finally realized that I had a serious injury, and they didn't want to fool around with it any longer.

I flew out to Los Angeles at the end of the week, fully prepared for another trip to the surgical suite. Intuition, I guess. I told my wife, "Don't expect me to be home for a little while." The pain was so bad that it couldn't just be swelling. Something had to be very wrong. Dr. Watkins agreed. He looked at my X rays, ordered another MRI, and then called me into his office and gave me the bad news. This time I was prepared. In fact, I was almost relieved. At least now I had proof: I really was injured.

I phoned Karen right away and asked her to come to L.A. Then I called my mom and asked if she could fly to Texas to watch the kids for a few days. She said "no problem," of course. That Thursday, November 14, I underwent back surgery for the third time in thirty-four months. As he had the first two times, Dr. Watkins removed a disk fragment; he also scraped away scar tissue that was putting pressure on some nerves. That's why I'd been having pain in my legs, as well as my back.

The surgery itself was no worse than any of the others I'd been through. Emotionally, though, I was shot. Dr. Watkins had made it quite clear that it was time for me to start thinking about doing something else with my life, while I was still healthy enough to walk. Although he couldn't be sure, he said it was likely that the injury had occurred in training camp. If so, I'd been playing with a herniated disk for the better part of *four months*. Had I known that, of course, it would have put a different spin on everything. Even I'm not crazy enough to go out on the football field when I know I have a herniated disk. But I had to endure another surgical procedure before anyone would tell me. The NFL is just a big game, man, especially when it comes to whether somebody is hurt or not. In the end, no one really gives a damn.

I went through a real bad time after I got back to Dallas. I moped around a lot, felt sorry for myself, drank too much. It hit me all of a sudden that this time I probably wasn't coming back. I didn't even have the will to come back—at least not right away. In addition to being totally wiped out physically, I was angry. I was bitter. Football had been my life for so long; the Cowboys had been my life. Before I went in to have surgery, I would have given my right leg for the chance to play again. But a lot of guys on the team, including guys I respect, were coming at me from all different angles, prodding me about playing. I'd tell them I couldn't, and they'd just stand there staring at me, telling me how bad I was needed. It was like they couldn't hear me or something. Or they didn't believe me. Damn! Didn't they know how much I wanted to play?

I understand the rules as well as anybody: No injury is too severe. I understand that I had a track record when it came to playing with pain. I always managed to get out on the field. But this time was different. The boys who knew me well should have understood. For them to start doing me like that, to start questioning me . . . man, that hurt. I'm not talking about everyone, mind you. A few of my closest friends—Leon Lett, Tony Tolbert, Godfrey Myles—were cool. But I lost respect for a lot of other people.

At home, my family was being very supportive. Princess would sit and read books to me for hours. C. J. would climb up on my lap and hug me. Even my littlest, Brianna, tried to help. The first time she saw me limping around with that back brace on, she looked like she thought I was from Mars. Pretty soon, though, she was rubbing my back, saying, "I'll make it better, Daddy."

She couldn't, though. I was in a funk. I wouldn't take calls from anyone, I wouldn't go out. Thankfully, Karen didn't pressure me. Instead, she worked behind the scenes to try to boost my spirits. She called a bunch of my friends who had already retired and asked them to call me, to let me know that there was life after football. Michael Carter, one of my teammates in San Francisco, came out to my house, because he couldn't get me on the phone. He just drove up and Karen let him in. Michael's a man of few words, but in his grumpy little way he tried to cheer me up. Eventually, Ronnie Lott got through to me, too. I didn't want to burden Ronnie, but the truth was, I needed to hear from him. He set me straight, just like always. He reminded me that there's more to life than money and football.

"You've accomplished a lot in this game," Ronnie said. "You shouldn't have any regrets. There's no reason to be mad—not when there's a whole world out there waiting for you."

He was right. It was time to look beyond the football field. When I had surgery in 1995, I started thinking about playing as soon as the anesthesia wore off. Not this time. There was no chance I was going to rush my rehabilitation just to suit up for one more playoff game. I'm not even sure I would have come back for another Super Bowl.

As it turned out, that wasn't something I had to worry about. Life was pretty miserable around the Ranch in '96. It seemed like things just kept getting worse. Suspensions, injuries, coaches who didn't know what the hell they were doing, players making excuses. It's amazing we made the playoffs at all.

Somehow, though, we did. We won three out of our last four regular-season games to sneak in. Then we beat the Vikings in a wild-card game. But that was it. A few days before we played the Carolina Panthers in a divisional playoff game, the story about Michael and Erik Williams blew up. And we'd already lost Leon for the rest of the year to a drug suspension. Suddenly the papers were full of stories about the crazy Cowboys again, about how we supposedly represented everything that was wrong with big-time professional sports in the '90s.

It seemed like the whole country wanted us to lose that game. And we did, 26–17. We got beat by a damn *expansion* team! Not a great way to go out. We deserved it, though. Despite all the people we were missing, we still had more talent than most of the teams in the league. But we didn't have the attitude. We didn't have the confidence. We were scared. And when you play scared . . . you lose.

Charles in Charge, Part XI
A FEW GOOD MEN

February 1997—

Once you hit thirty in the NFL, they say you're getting old—even if you're healthy. Chances are, though, if you've played seven or eight years of professional football, you're not healthy. And each time you get injured, you lose a step or two. Me and Father Time have been in a big old fight the last few years. It's fairly obvious by now that he's winning. That's life, I guess.

My wife doesn't want me to play anymore. She's afraid I'm going to end up crippled, so she's been mapping out my whole life, figuring out ways to keep me busy after I retire. Dr. Watkins has strongly advised me not to play again. He's not trying to scare me or anything; he just wants me to realize that I have a very good chance of herniating another disk. My back is weakened, and there's not much I can do about it. Of course, that's just the doctor's suggestion. It's still my decision. As of right now, I don't know what I'm going to do. Everyone's telling me to retire; I probably *should* retire. The thing is . . . I still love this fucking game.

My body is starting to recover. I'm feeling better. When that happens, I get the itch to play. But I don't want to fade out like some pathetic old-timer—one of those guys who only comes in on third down to rush the passer and then has to suck oxygen on the bench for the next ten minutes. I refuse to let that happen. That's not the way I want to be remembered. I need to feel the heat of the game, the emotion. I need to be out there every play . . . tasting it . . . living it. If I can't be a complete player, I won't play at all.

———————

I'm not sure how I'll handle not being an athlete. I have a lot of anger in my soul. As a football player, I funnel that rage onto the field; I use it in a positive way. What do I do with it now? I've lost my temper around the house a few times in the last couple months. I've broken a door. That's no way to be. If I retire, I'll need help dealing with the stress. If that means going through counseling, then that's what I'll do. People have been trying to get me to see psychologists all my life, and I've always fought it. This time, though, it might not be such a bad idea.

Then again, maybe I'll just throw myself into something else. I always thought I would have made a great soldier. A Marine. Maybe a Green Beret . . . or an officer in Special Services. It would be an incredible physical and mental challenge. I'd love doing shit like that —learning different techniques for taking people out, surviving with nothing more than your wits and your bare hands; relying totally on yourself.

Karen laughs when I talk about that. She says I wouldn't even get through boot camp. In fact, she doesn't think I'd last a week in the military. "You can't take orders," she says. "The man would tell you to shine his shoes and you'd be out the door."

She's got a point there. I don't like being told what to eat, what to wear, how to talk. That shit would drive me crazy. But the other stuff—the *spy* stuff—that would be kind of fun. I'd like that.

I don't know, man . . . I guess I'm just a dreamer. But that's okay. I figure we all deserve a break from reality once in a while. Life is no fun if you can't dream.

CHARLES HALEY

Number:	94
Height:	6-5
Weight:	255
Birthplace:	Gladys, Va.
Birth Date:	1/6/64
College:	James Madison '86

Career Statistics

Solo Tackles:	398
Assisted Tackles:	113
Total Tackles:	511
Sacks:	97.5
Quarterback Pressures:	160
Interceptions:	2
Pass Deflections:	38
Fumbles Forced:	25
Fumbles Recovered:	7

Career Highlights

- NCAA Division I-AA All-America: 1985
- Selected to NFL Pro Bowl: 1988, 1990, 1991, 1994, 1995
- Named All-Pro: 1990, 1994
- NFC Defensive Player of the Year: 1990
- Only player in NFL history to win five Super Bowl rings: 1988, 1989, 1992, 1993, 1995

About the Author

Charles Haley is one of the most accomplished defensive players in the National Football League. A fierce competitor and gifted athlete, he grew up in rural Virginia and became a Division I-AA All-American at James Madison University. During a stellar ten-year professional career with the San Francisco 49ers and Dallas Cowboys, he has played in five Pro Bowls and twice been named All-Pro. In 1991 he was named National Football Conference Defensive Player of the Year. Widely regarded as one of the game's greatest pass rushers, Charles is the only player in league history to have won five Super Bowl rings.

Joe Layden, a former newspaper columnist and editor, is the author of more than a dozen books, including *America on Wheels: The First 100 Years, Notre Dame Football—A to Z,* and *Women in Sport.* His work has been honored by the New York Newspaper Publishers Association, the Associated Press Sports Editors, and the New York State Associated Press Association. He lives in Saratoga Springs, New York, with his wife, Susan, and their daughter, Emily.